NATIONAL GALLERY SINGAPORE

Art in Singapore since the 19th Cer

SIAPA NAMA KAMU?

SELECTIONS FROM THE EXHIBITION

Published in conjunction with

SIAPA NAMA KAMU?
Art in Singapore since the 19th Century

an exhibition organised by the National Gallery Singapore.

Published in 2015

Please direct all enquiries to the publisher at:
National Gallery Singapore
1 St. Andrew's Road, #01-01, Singapore 178957

Cover image
Chua Mia Tee. *National Language Class*. 1959.
Oil on canvas, 112 × 153 cm.

Editor: Sara Siew
Editorial Assistant: Rayne Ngoi
Designer: Hjgher

National Library Board, Singapore Cataloguing in Publication Data

Names: Siew, Sara, 1986– editor. National Gallery Singapore, publisher.
Title: Siapa Nama Kamu? : Art in Singapore since the 19th Century :
Selections from the Exhibition / Editor, Sara Siew.
Description: Singapore : National Gallery Singapore, 2015.
Identifiers: OCN925506378 | ISBN 978-981-09-7384-1 (paperback)
Subjects: LCSH: Art, Singaporean--19th century--Exhibitions. | Art, Singaporean--20th century--Exhibitions. | Art, Singaporean--21st century --Exhibitions. | Art--Singapore--History.

Classification: LCC N7330.S5 | DDC 709.5957074--dc23

Contents

Foreword

EUGENE TAN
Director, National Gallery Singapore

The opening of the National Gallery Singapore comes at a time of great significance for Singapore, in her fiftieth year of independence. What is the relationship of art to a nation like Singapore? This is one of the key questions that the exhibition Siapa Nama Kamu? seeks to address. The titular phrase, which means "What is your name?" in Malay, can be found in a work featured in the exhibition, *National Language Class* by Chua Mia Tee. *National Language Class* was painted in 1959, the year Singapore gained self-governance from the British, and has since come to resonate with that historical moment. In it, a group of Chinese students are shown learning Malay, the national language of Singapore. The question *Siapa Nama Kamu?* is scribbled on the chalkboard in front of them—while hardly incongruous in such a scene, this is perhaps also a provocation to viewers to consider the parameters of personal and national identity, and how they relate to art in Singapore.

While Singapore has been an independent nation for fifty years, she has been a site for the production of art for much longer. The story of art in Singapore that Siapa Nama Kamu? presents begins in the 19th century and continues till today. A survey of this scale naturally engenders a host of questions: How does one begin to understand Singapore art? Are there shared experiences that connect artists in Singapore? What are the key impulses that drive the production and reception of art in Singapore? How are we able to tell a history of Singapore through Singapore art? How is Singapore art connected with regional and global art developments? This exhibition seeks to address such questions, while fostering new discussion and thought on these issues.

Siapa Nama Kamu? features more than 400 artworks, each significant in its own respect. As such, selecting the 100 works for this exhibition album was a challenging task. This selection will, nevertheless, present in broad strokes the curatorial narrative of the exhibition, drawing attention to its themes and concerns while presenting the evolution of art in Singapore in chronological fashion. These works hail from the National Collection as well as external collections; the presence of the latter attests to the generosity and understanding of individuals and institutions around the world who have aided in our endeavour, and to whom we convey our deepest gratitude.

It is my hope that this album will function as an extension of one's experience of the National Gallery Singapore and our collection; in so doing, it will ideally foster a greater understanding of the development of art in Singapore. It is also a record, albeit abbreviated, of an exhibition that is of great significance to Singapore, one that has been long in the making.

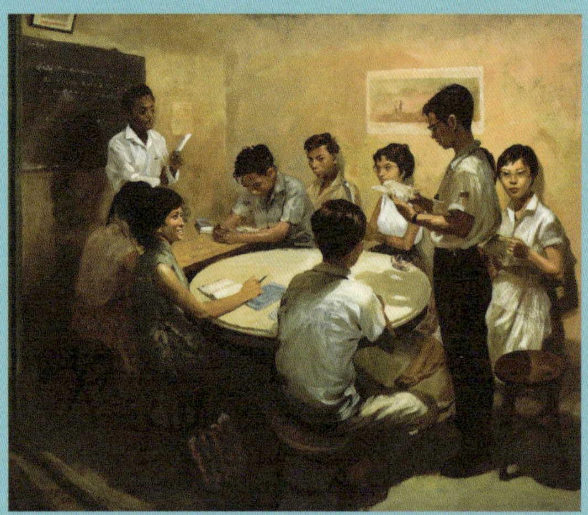

Chua Mia Tee
National Language Class
1959
Oil on canvas
112 × 153 cm

Introduction

The most arresting fact about Singapore is her location: set in a vast archipelago of island neighbours, she raises questions of scale and proportion whenever she is contemplated. Seeming almost submerged in the immensity of their surroundings, Singapore's sea-locked inhabitants are constantly compelled to look outwards.

Encounters between Singapore and the world at large have informed the development of art in Singapore since the 19th century, when much of Southeast Asia was under European colonial rule. With diverse, external values and systems coming into close contact with the region's existing beliefs and social structures, the 19th century represents a break with a past continuum. It also marks the beginning of the modern condition and the rise of modern art in Southeast Asia and Singapore.

These developments, and the complexities therein, form the focus of the exhibition Siapa Nama Kamu? Art in Singapore since the 19th Century. The titular question, which in Malay means what is your name, may be found in the work *National Language Class*. Created in 1959, the year Singapore gained self-governance from the British, this painting hung on the walls of the City Hall in the 1960s where the Ministry of Culture was located. It has come to resonate with that point in Singapore's history, while at the same time provoking questions about the artist's individual response to his surroundings and circumstances.

Siapa Nama Kamu? is then a question and an invitation—to consider how art can mirror, but also complicate, our reality.

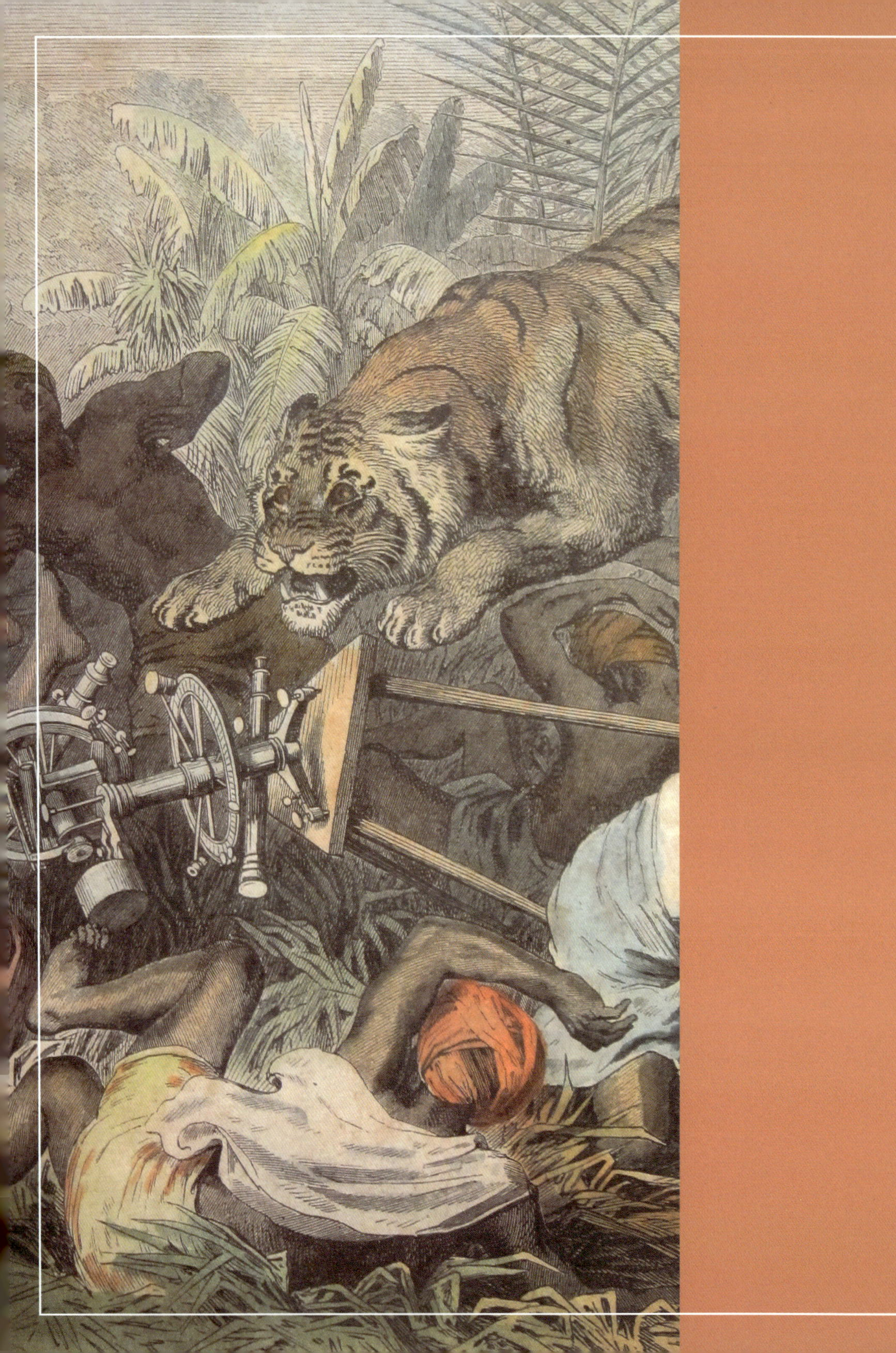

Tropical Tapestry

The year is 1835. A group of labourers, led by the architect and government official G.D. Coleman, is building a road through the jungles of Singapore. In an instant the menacing silence of the jungle is broken—a tiger lunges out of the impenetrable vegetation, throwing the men into a fevered frenzy. Although tigers had been connected to tales in the Malay world from as early as the 14th century, when Singapore was known as Temasek, the notion of untold dangers lurking in Singapore's jungles still captured public imagination.

Coleman's encounter with Singapore, like many others, informed some of the earliest visual representations of the island. From 1819, sojourners and settlers arrived at the shores of this young British colony. Their encounters resulted in a vivid tropical tapestry of impressions, from maps and landscapes to natural history drawings. While new images were created, there were also pre-existing pictorial traditions—sculptures, decorated manuscripts, and textiles of indigenous communities in the region.

In the 19th century, several tropical motifs started to take root, and were circulated through prints and photographs. By the early 20th century, Singapore's growing affluence created a demand for artists to produce works for public and private patrons, marking the beginnings of modern art in Singapore.

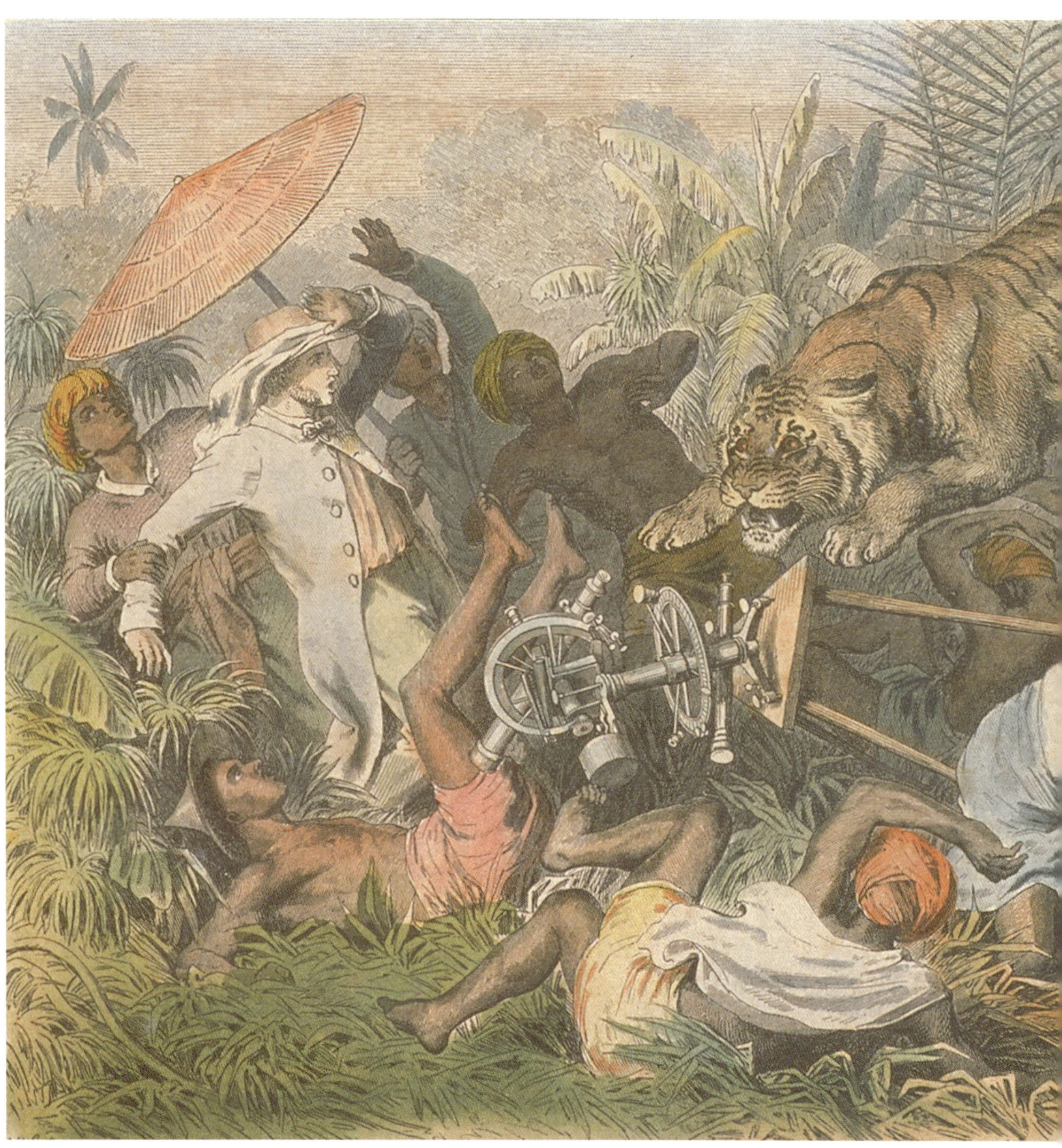

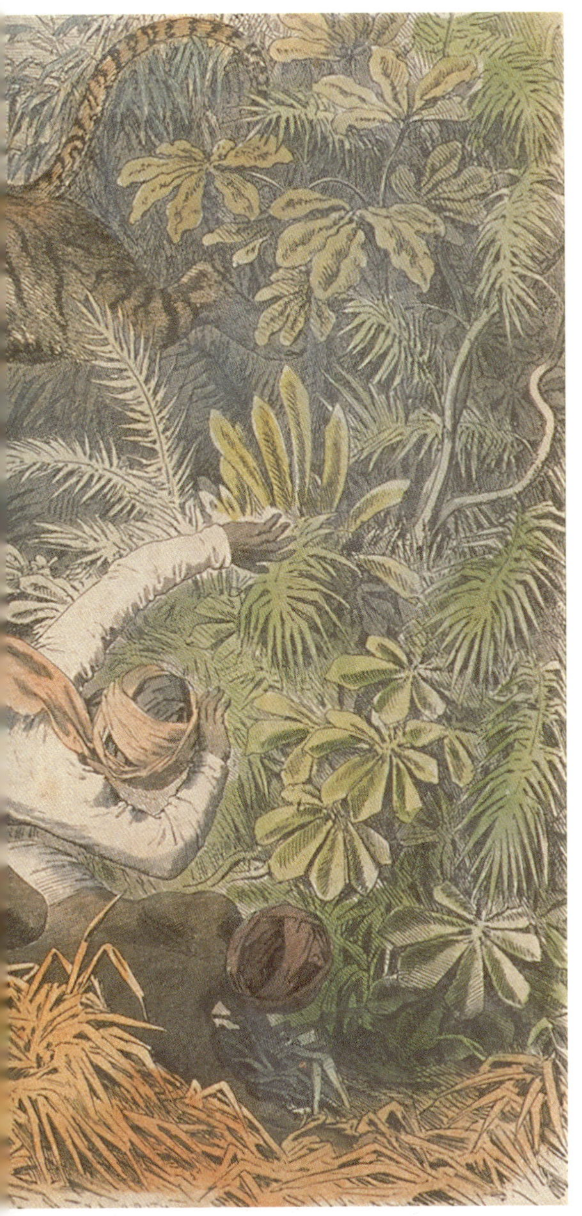

Tiger sightings were common in 1830s Singapore. This print is an imaginative retelling of colonial architect G.D. Coleman's road surveying trip in 1835 and his group's encounter with a tiger. The swift ferocity of the attacking tiger hints at dangers lurking beneath the unexplored terrain of Singapore's tropical jungles. As a fantastical image, this print invites us to think about how Singapore was imagined in the 19th century.

Heinrich Leutemann. *Unterbrochene Straßenmessung auf Singapore (Interrupted Road Surveying in Singapore)*. c. 1865. Wood engraving, 20.8 × 29.4 cm. Collection of National Museum of Singapore.

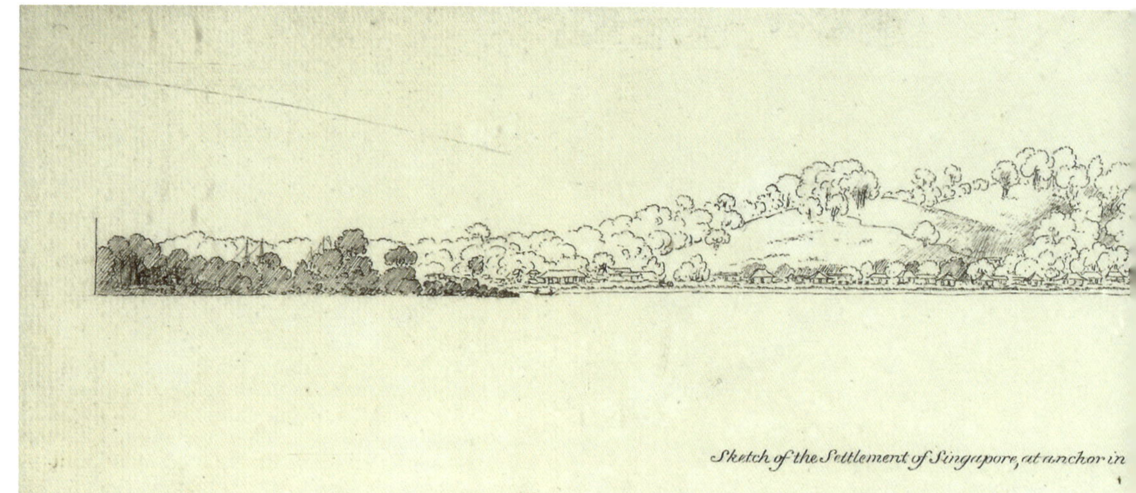

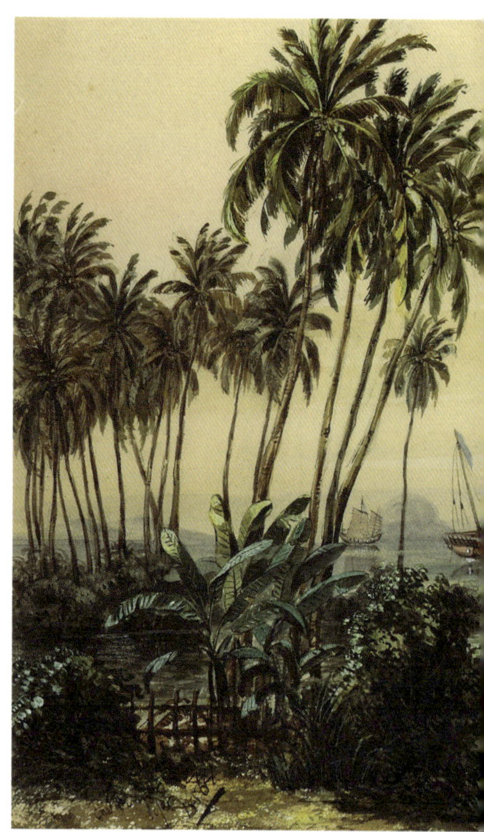

Charles Henry Cazalet
Malay Huts, MacPherson Bridge
1856
Watercolour and pencil on paper
34 × 73 cm

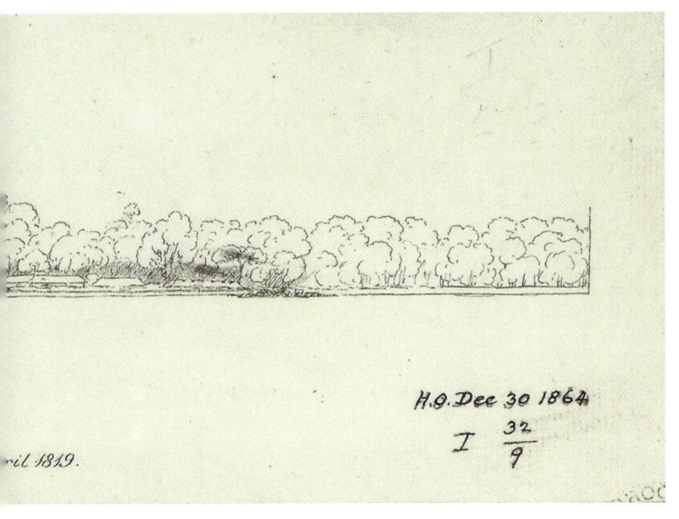

In 1819, Sir Stamford Raffles tasked two Bombay Marine vessels to conduct a coastal survey while he went ashore to meet with the Temenggong. In an age preceding photography, draughtsmen were tasked to create drawings on marine expeditions. These drawings are some of the earliest visual impressions of contact between the British and the local community, a possible precursor to the harbour view scenes that became iconic in 19th-century representations of Singapore.

Artist unknown. *Sketch of the Settlement of Singapore, at anchor in 4 fathoms*. April 1819. Hand-drawn sketch in black and brown ink on paper, 11 × 44 cm. Collection of the National Archives, UK, ADM 344/1300.

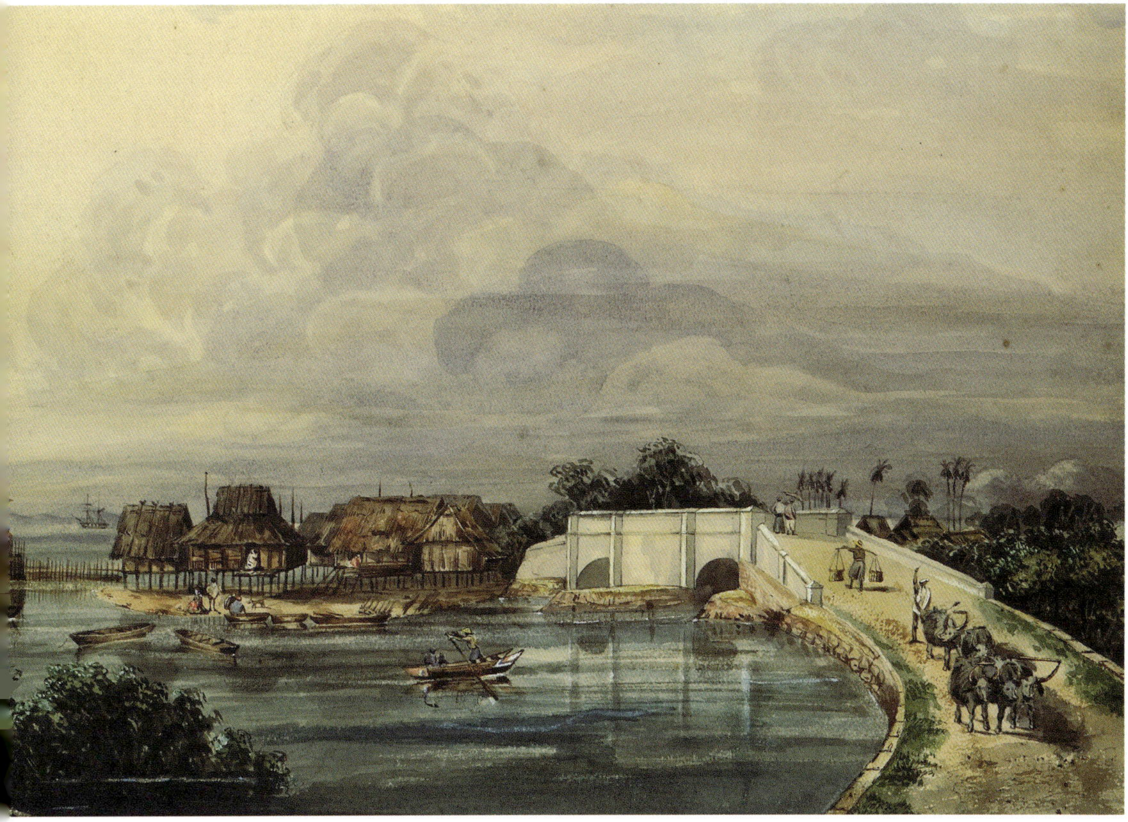

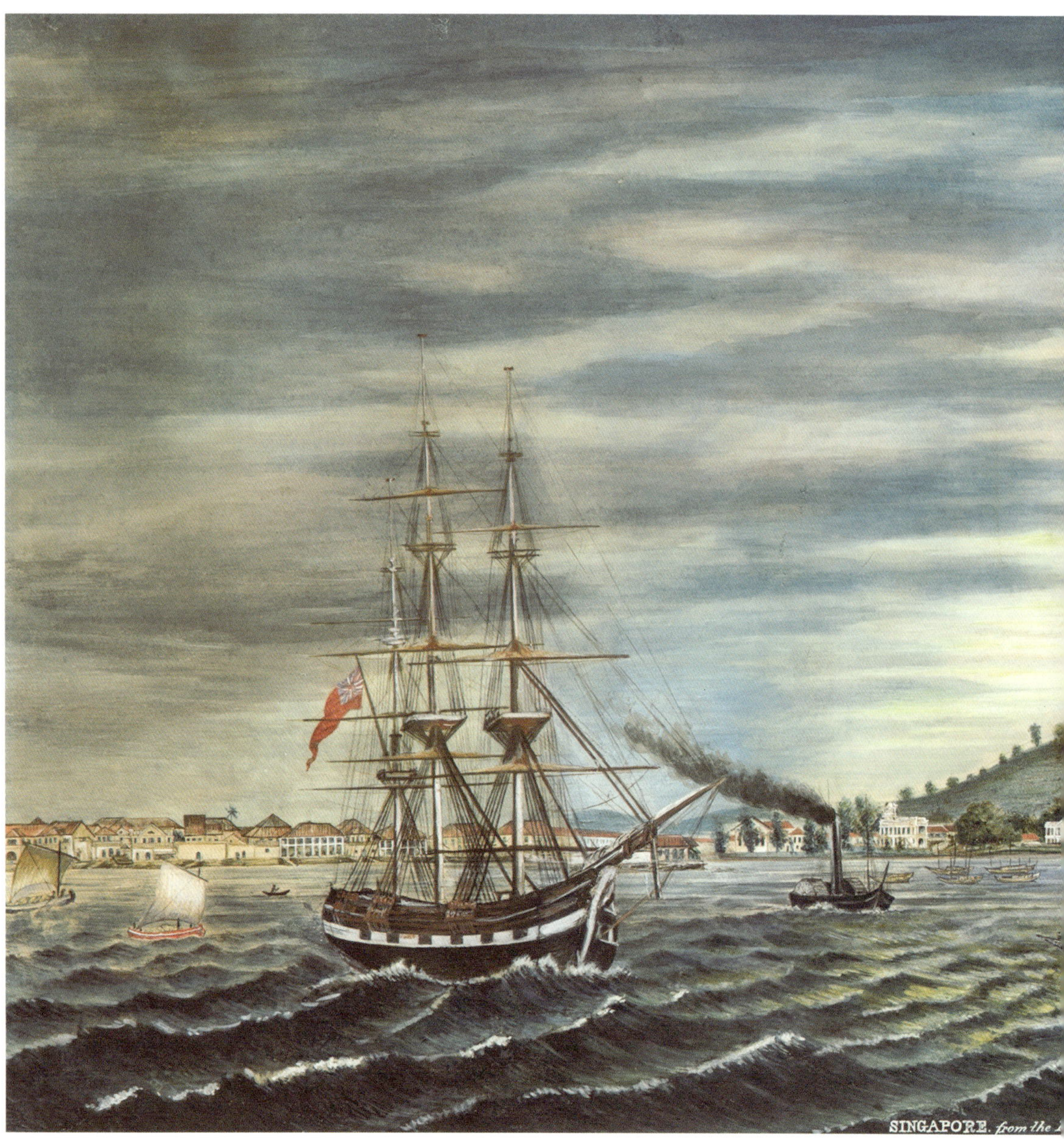
SINGAPORE. from the

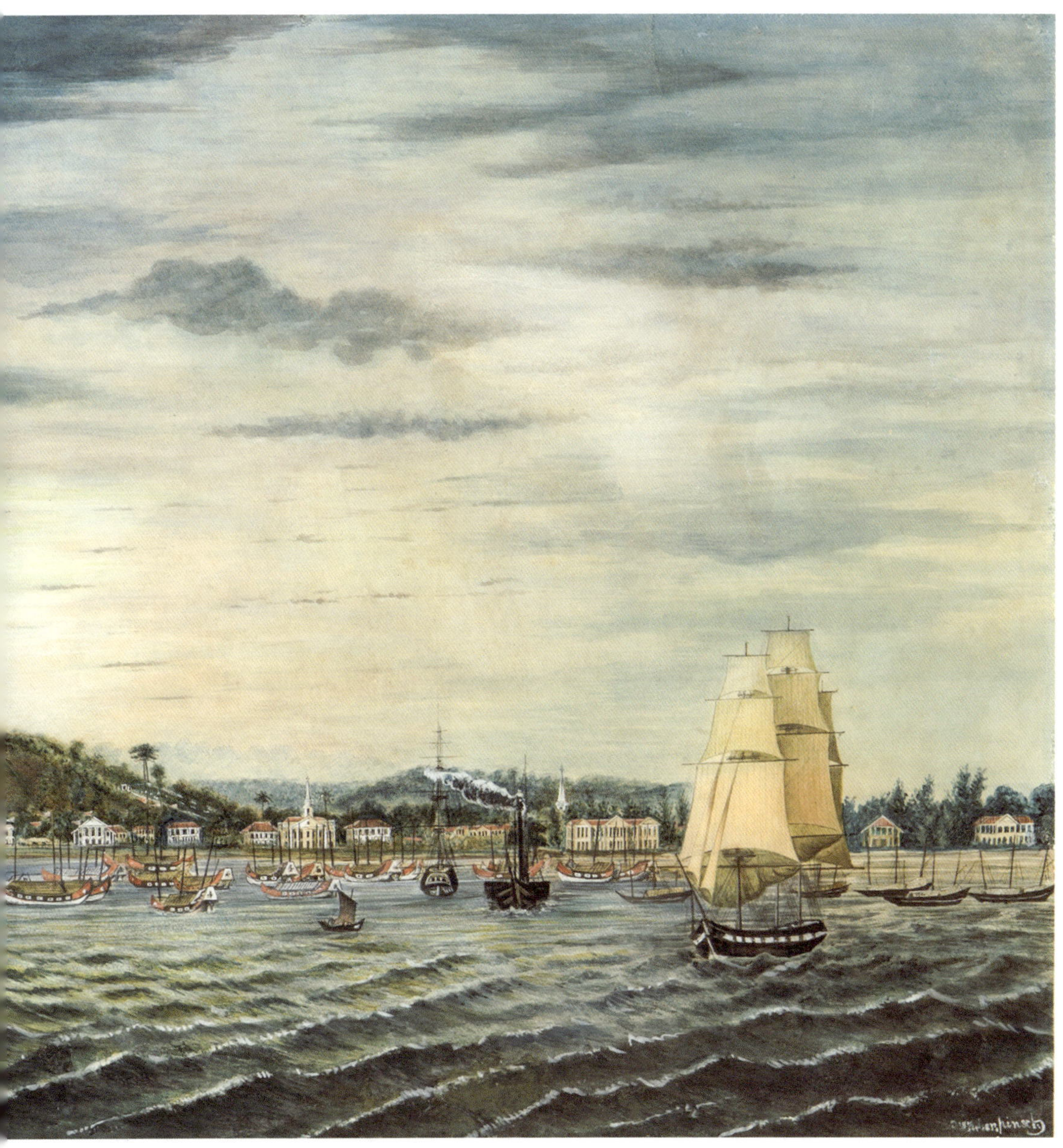

This waterfront view of Singapore typifies how early settlers perceived the island as a trading port. For those who arrived via the sea, their first sight of Singapore was likely that of its bustling port and the busy river that connected people to the jungles inland. The depiction of Singapore's connection to sea and river is a recurring motif in paintings of the colony from the 19th century.

Robert Wilson Wiber. *Panoramic View of Singapore from the Harbour.* 1849. Watercolour and gouache on paper, 32 × 67.5 cm.

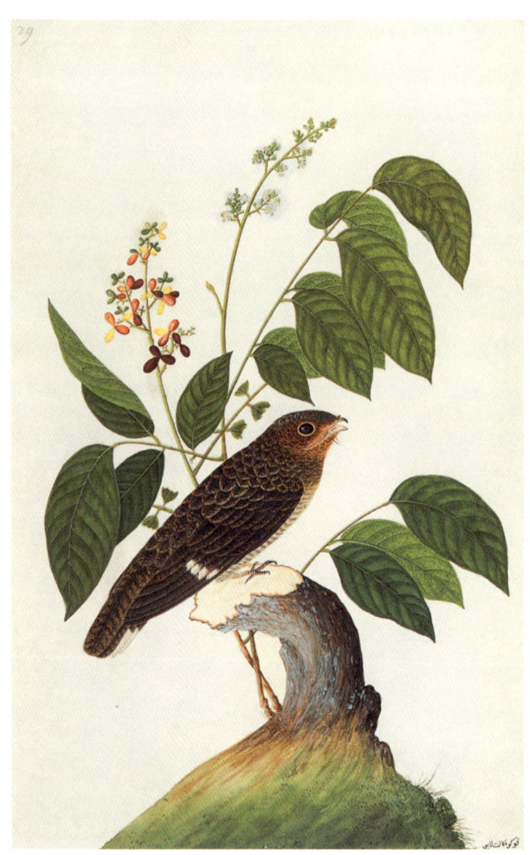

Artist unknown. *Dusky Broadbill, Takau Besar (Corydon sumatranus).* 1803–1818. Watercolour on paper, 46.5 × 29.5 cm. Gift of GK Goh. Collection of National Museum of Singapore.

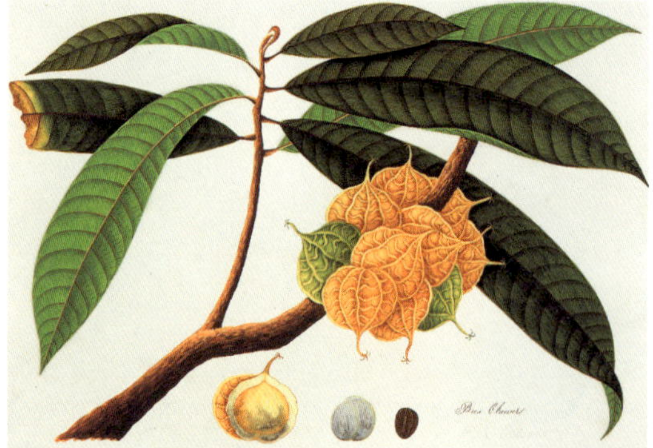

Artist unknown. *Mendaroh (Ptychopyxis costata).* 1803–1818. Watercolour on paper, 37.6 × 54.2 cm. Gift of GK Goh. Collection of National Museum of Singapore.

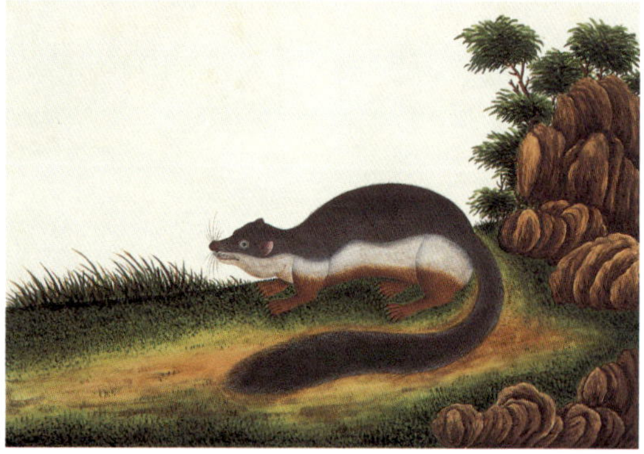

Artist unknown. *Prevost's Squirrel, Tupai Gading (Callosciurus prevostii).* 1803–1818. Watercolour on paper, 38 × 54.5 cm. Gift of GK Goh. Collection of National Museum of Singapore.

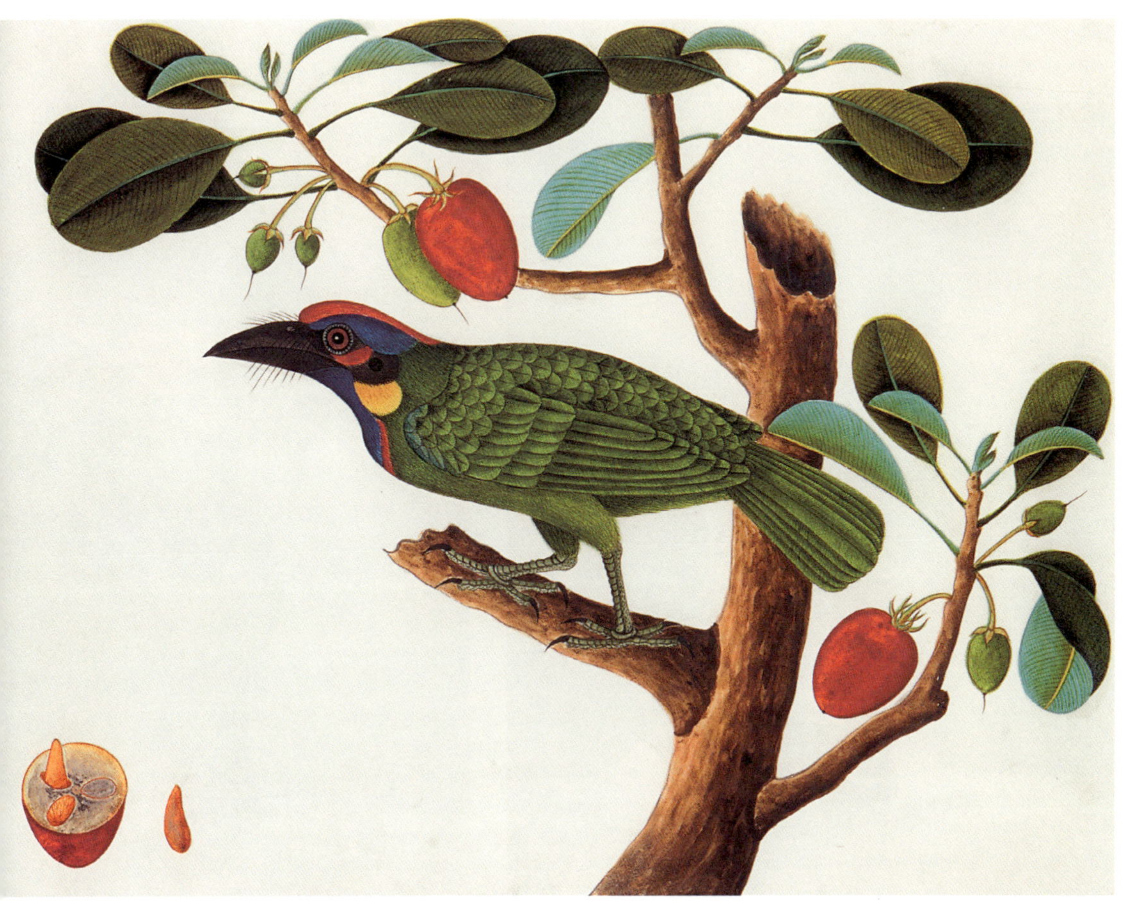

Red-crowned Barbet was commissioned sometime between 1803 and 1818 by William Farquhar, then Resident of Malacca, as part of a scientific survey of flora and fauna in the Straits Settlements. It is, however, more than just a natural history drawing. The harmonious medley of colours and precise details in each brushstroke create a lively portrayal of the bird, revealing the aesthetic impulses of the unknown Chinese artist.

Artist unknown. *Red-crowned Barbet, Burung Takur Mahkota Merah (Megalaima rafflesii)*. 1803–1818. Watercolour on paper, 38.2 × 54.4 cm. Gift of GK Goh. Collection of National Museum of Singapore.

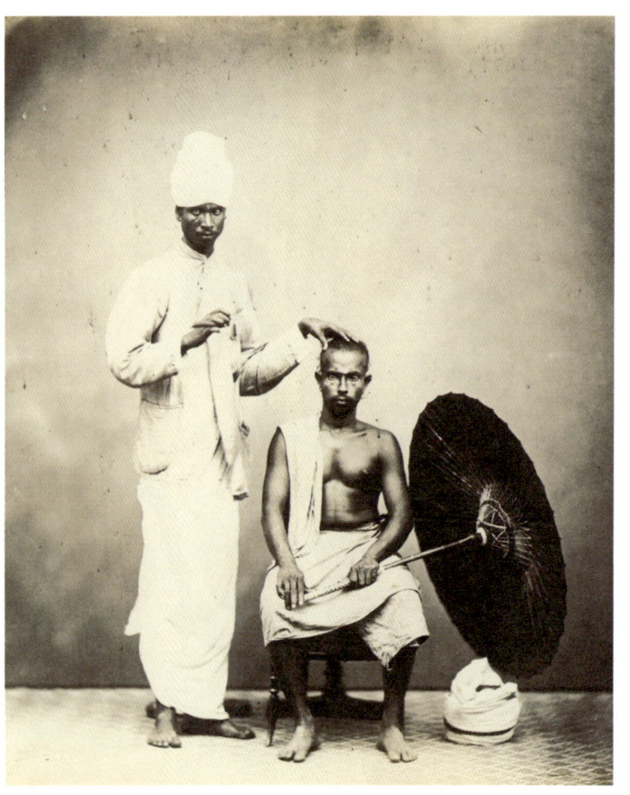

A. Sachtler & Co.
Untitled (*Two Indian Men*)
c. 1863–1872
Albumen print
27 × 22 cm
Collection of Mr and Mrs Lee Kip Lee

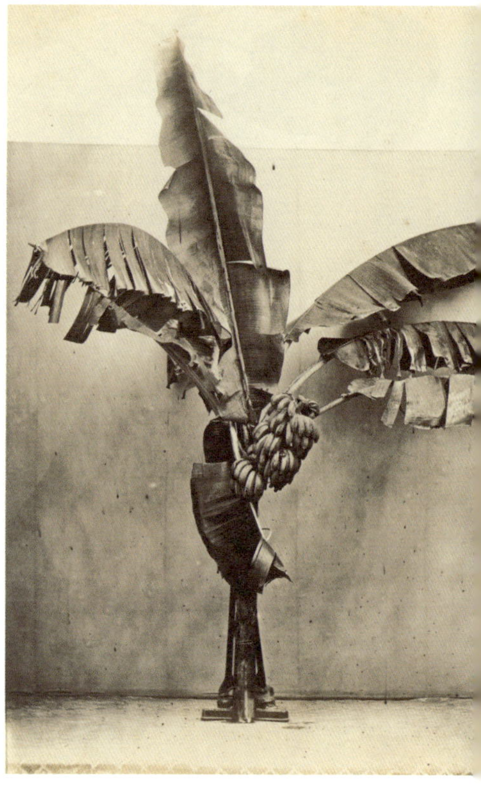

A. Sachtler & Co.
Untitled (*Banana Plant*)
c. 1863–1872
Albumen print
28.5 × 25.2 cm
Collection of Mr and Mrs Lee Kip Lee

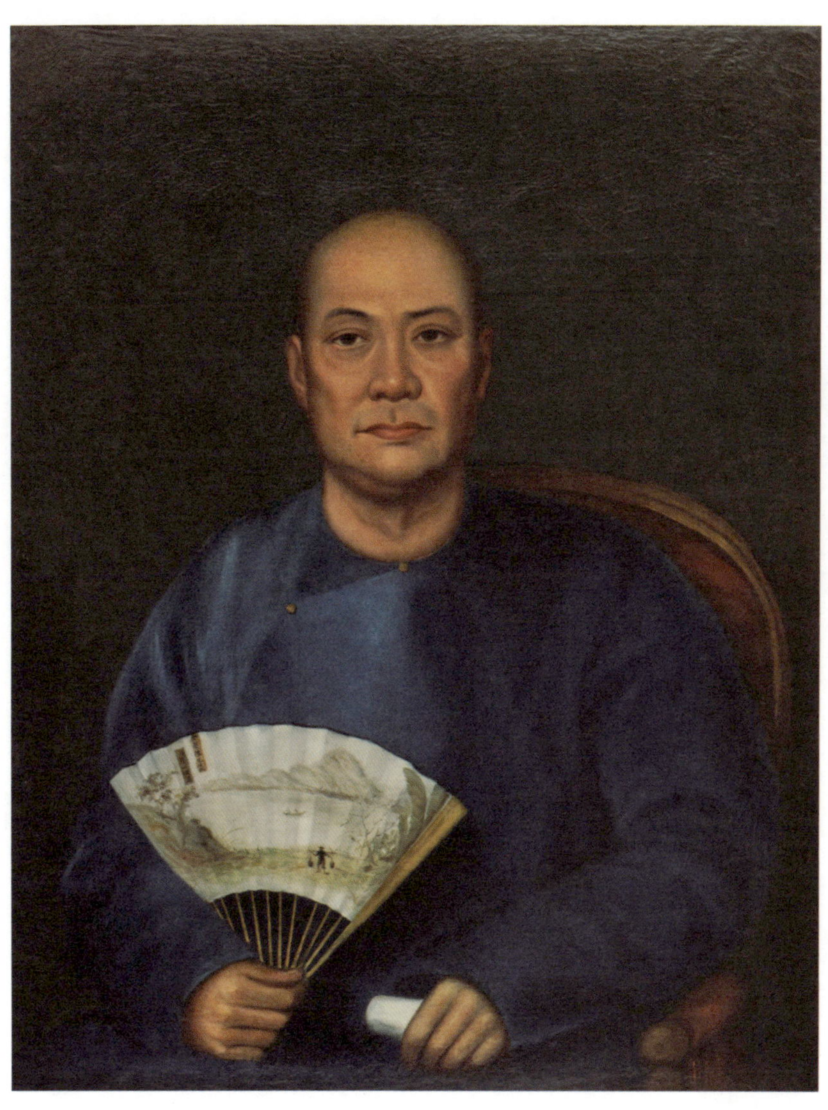

Luo Yi Hu
Portrait of Tan Kim Seng
Undated
Oil on canvas
97 × 76 cm
Gift of Winston Tan in memory of Edward Tan Tiang Leong
Collection of National University of Singapore Museum

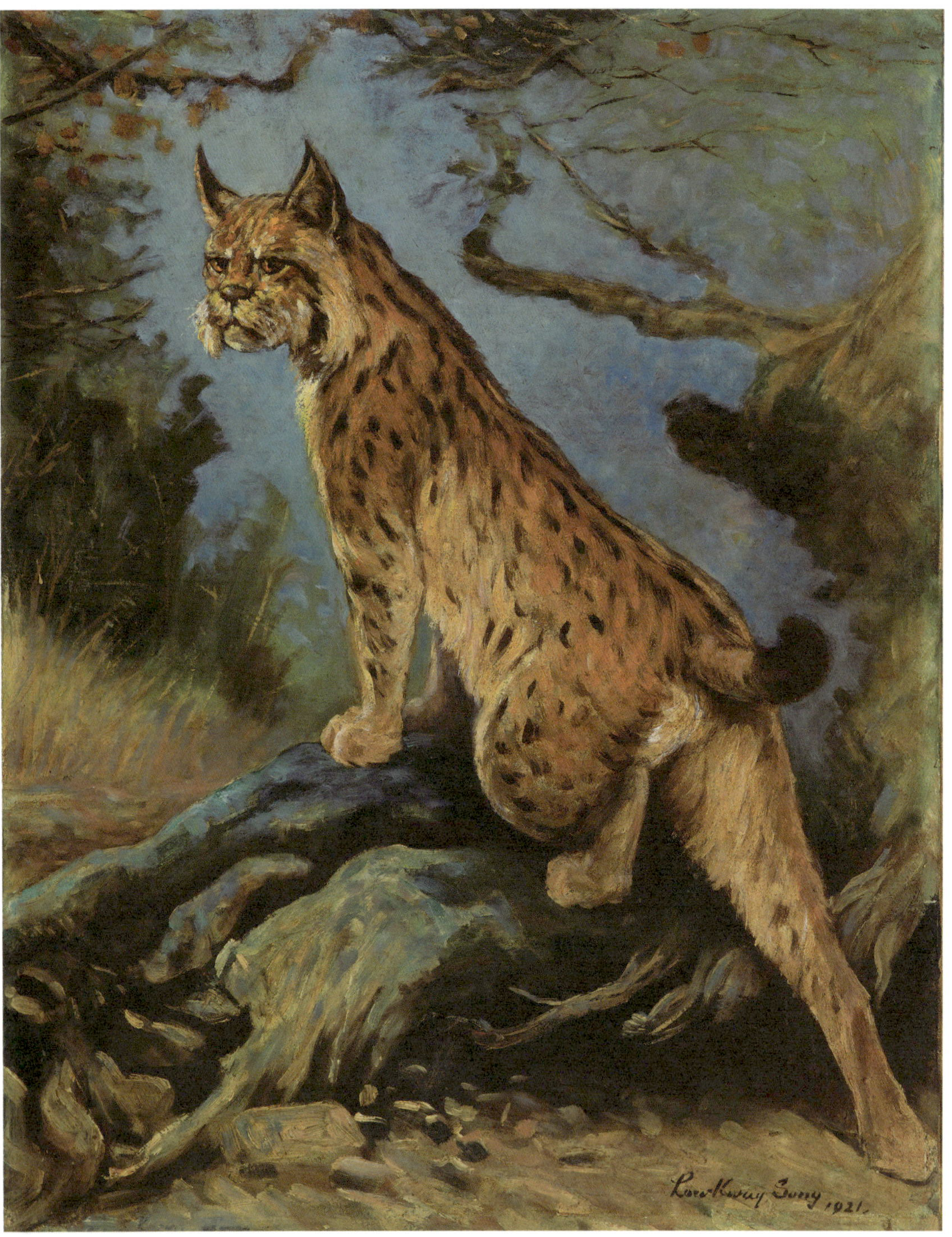
1921.

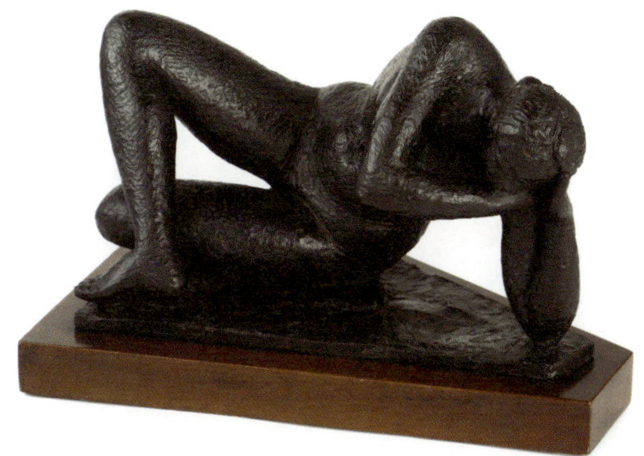

Dora Gordine
Serene Jade
1949
Bronze
21 × 35 × 30 cm
Gift of Elizabeth Choy

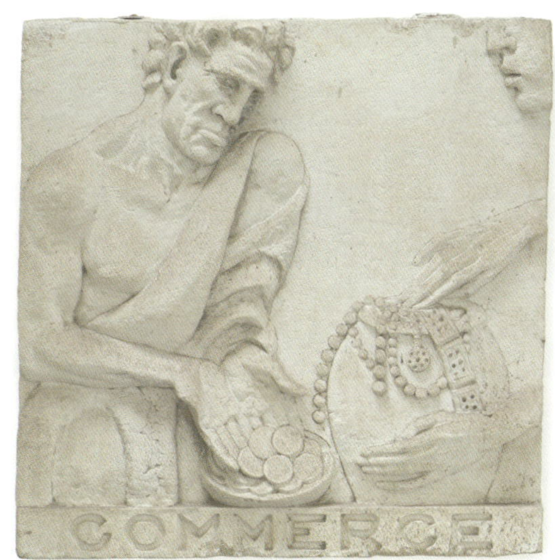

Rudolfo Nolli
Relief from Nunes Building, Malacca Street: Commerce
c. 1930s
Stone
91 × 92 × 9.5 cm
Collection of Dr Kenson Kwok

OPPOSITE PAGE

This depiction of a lynx—a solitary wild cat found in Europe and Central Asia—is one of the earliest known surviving examples of an oil painting by a Singapore artist. Low Kway Song was the epitome of an artist who was not constrained by borders. He established a successful photography studio, worked as a commercial illustrator, and produced high-profile commissioned portraits, creating works as he travelled around the region.

Low Kway Song. *Lynx*. 1921. Oil on canvas, 58.5 × 45 cm. Collection of Low Keong Hee Richard & Low Keong Ann Arthur.

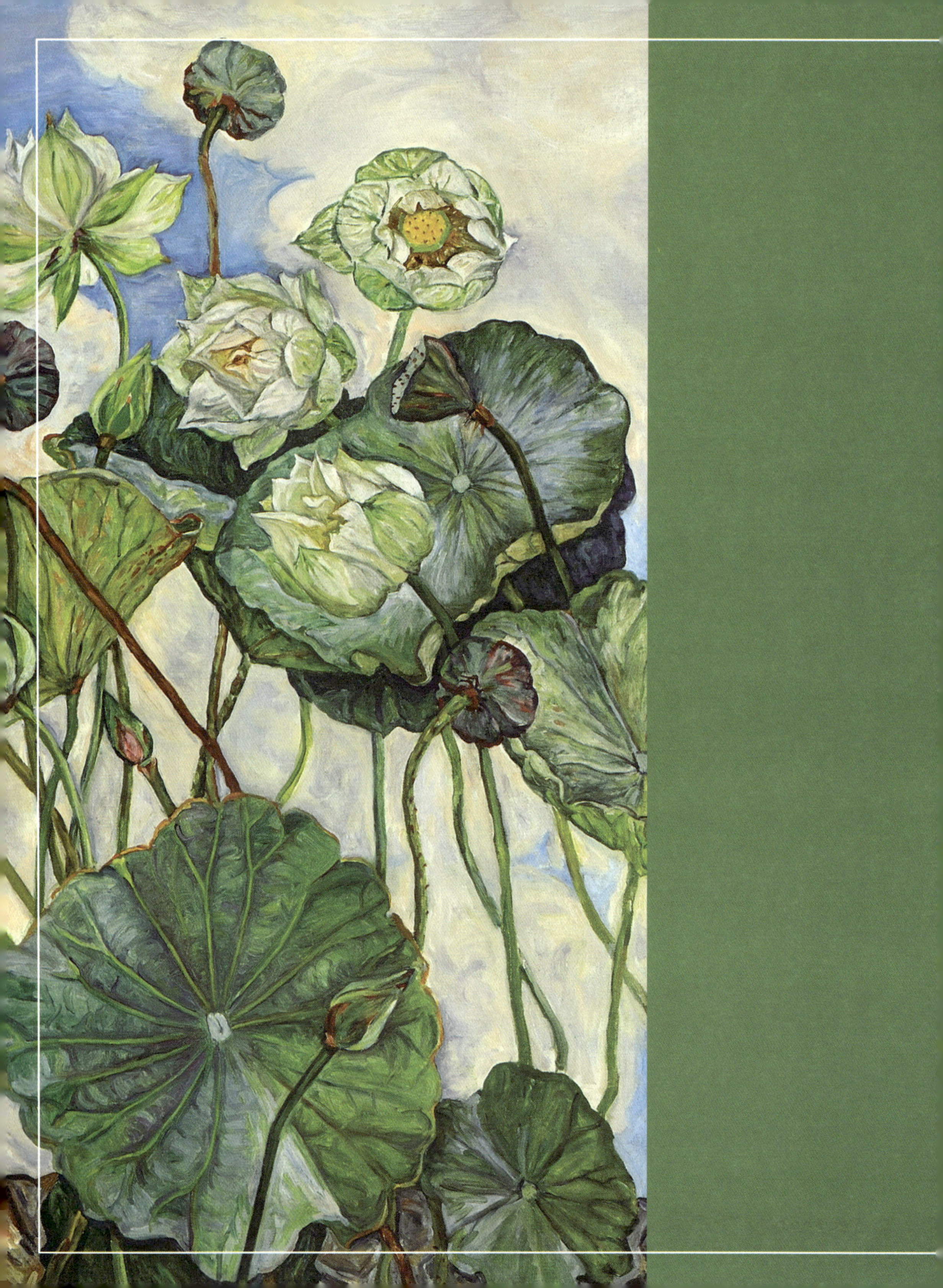

Nanyang Reverie

When he founded the Nanyang Academy of Fine Arts in 1938, Lim Hak Tai strongly believed that "art should have a sense of localness" and hoped that the academy could help to "propagate art with Nanyang characteristics."

Nanyang, or the South Seas, was originally used by Chinese maritime traders to refer to the Southeast Asian region located south of China. To Lim, however, Nanyang was not merely a geographical reference but the basis of a new art that reflected the realities of its locale. Although the idea of a Nanyang art first emerged among local Chinese writers in the 1930s, this movement soon encompassed visual artists who sought to infuse their works with a local identity. What they encountered—local landscapes, peoples, cultural motifs—became their subject matter; indigenous materials and techniques, like batik, were incorporated into art-making as well.

The desire to develop an artistic language distinct to the region continued to be evident in the 1950s and 1960s, following the stymied rate of artistic production during the Japanese Occupation. Artists and artist groups—like the Society of Malay Artists and Ten Men Art Group—travelled around Southeast Asia, providing a range of perspectives on the concept of Nanyang; a pronounced instance is the trip made by Chen Chong Swee, Chen Wen Hsi, Cheong Soo Pieng and Liu Kang to Bali in 1952. This trip inspired new subject matter and fresh approaches to the four artists' works, which were exhibited a year later. The success of the 1953 exhibition, as well as the formalistic innovations it featured, was to make an indelible mark on modern art in Singapore. Despite this it may be said that the Nanyang movement remained an organic one into the 1970s, with no prescribed method, style or manifesto—only the impression of a tropical site encountered and idealised.

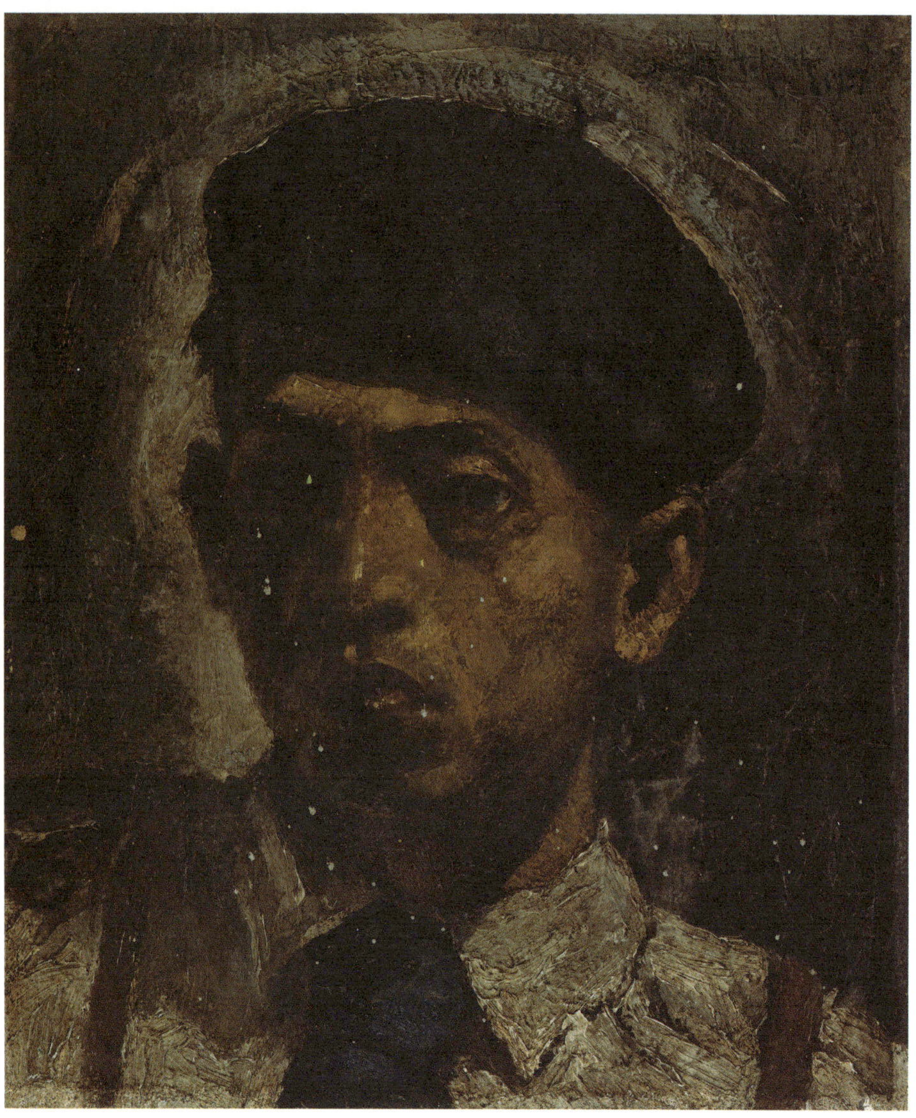

This self-portrait was likely created when the artist was studying art in France in the 1920s, its muted colours and rough, expressive brushwork reminiscent of the School of Paris paintings. When Tchang Ju Chi settled in Singapore in 1927, he married these stylistic influences with local subject matter, effectively engaging with the idea of a Nanyang art. Tchang was a co-founder of the Society of Chinese Artists, one of the earliest art societies in Singapore.

Tchang Ju Chi. *Untitled* (*Self Portrait*). 1937. Oil on canvas, 36 × 30 cm. Collection of Chang Si Fun (Shewin Chang).

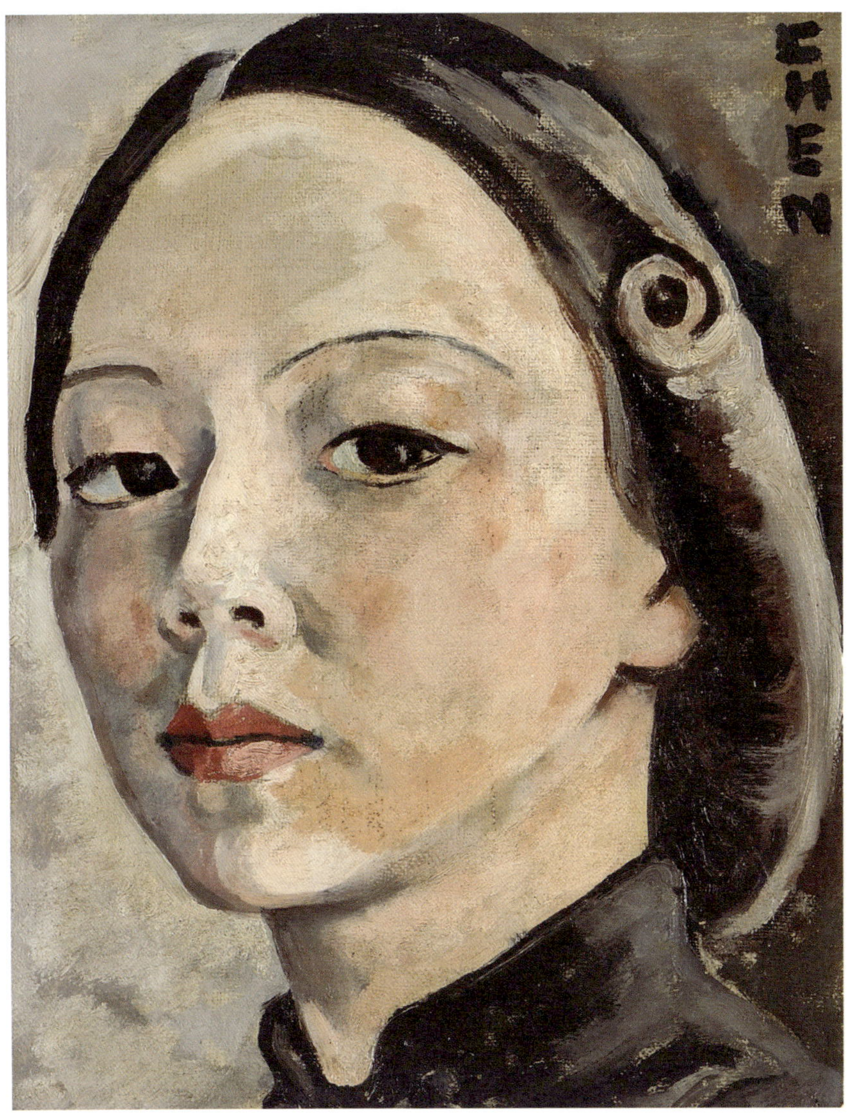

This self-portrait was made by Georgette Chen not long after her husband, Eugene Chen, passed away. Georgette's features are expressed in warm tones, succinct contours and subtle brushwork, making for a compelling portrait of one of the most prominent woman artists in Singapore art history, while hinting at her stoicism and dignity in the aftermath of World War II.

Georgette Chen. *Self Portrait*. c. 1946. Oil on canvas, 22.5 × 17.5 cm. Gift of Lee Foundation.

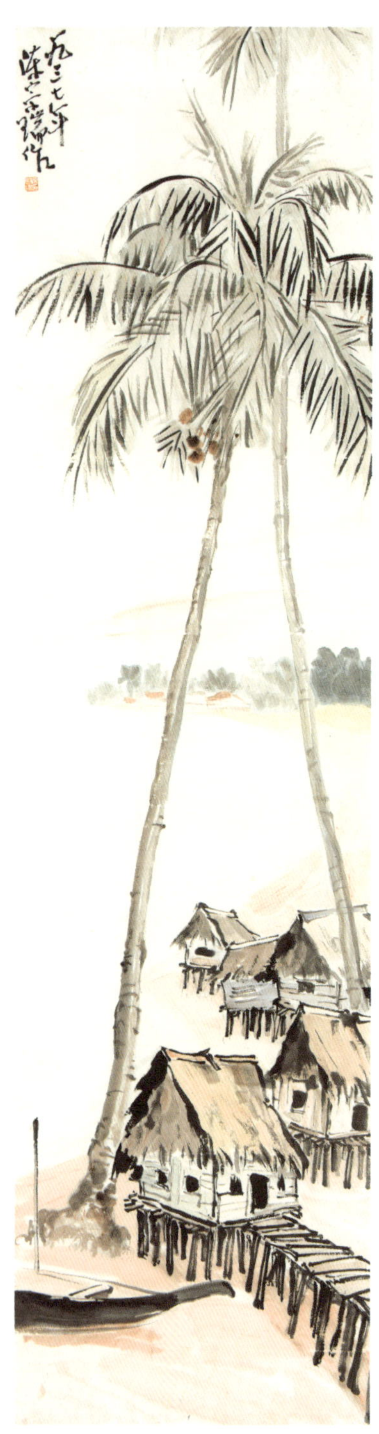

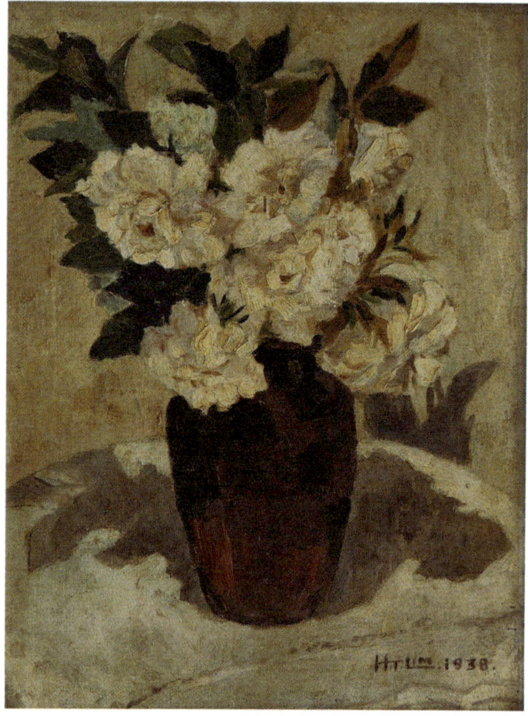

This is the earliest surviving work by China-born artist Lim Hak Tai. It was painted in 1938, the year he became founding principal of the Nanyang Academy of Fine Arts. The academy, which is today Singapore's oldest tertiary arts school, offered courses in sketching, watercolour and oil painting, and Chinese ink painting. This work is typical of the still-life compositions that would have been taught in the classroom.

Lim Hak Tai. *Still Life—Flowers*. 1938. Oil on board, 40.5 × 30.5 cm.

Chen Chong Swee
Kampong Scene
1937
Chinese ink and colour on paper
153 × 40.5 cm
Gift of the family of the late Chen Chong Swee

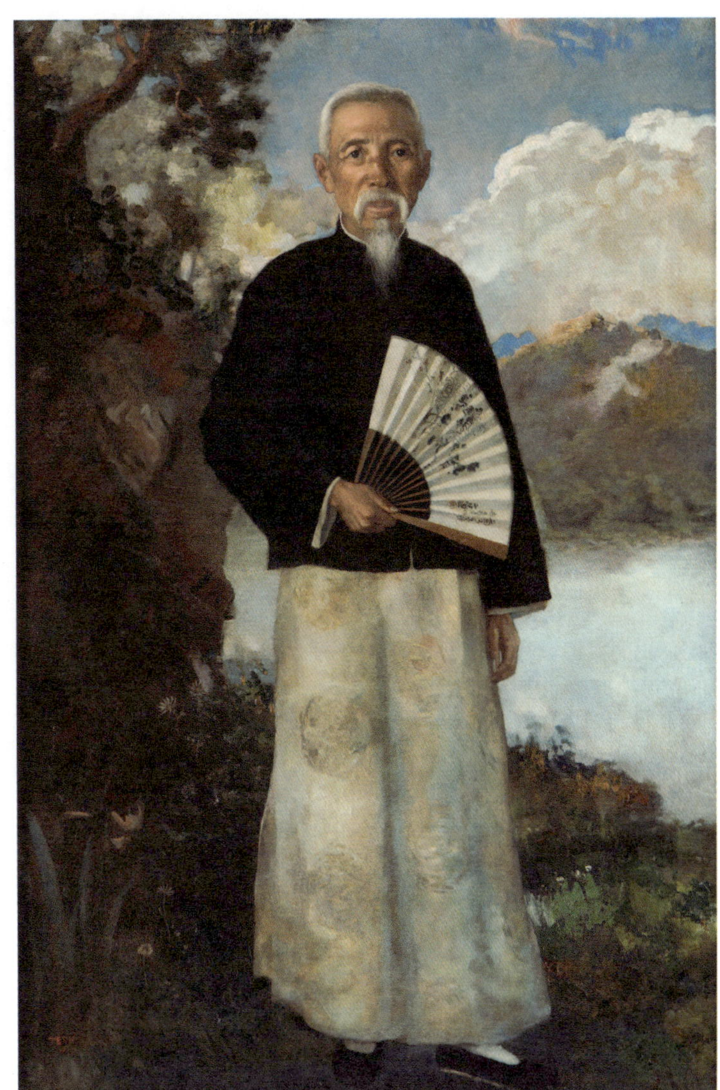

This life-like portrait of Singapore entrepreneur Lim Chee Gee, also known as Lim Loh, was painted by Xu Beihong. Trained in Europe, Xu advocated using scientific realism and the direct study of nature to rejuvenate Chinese painting. Apart from his influence on local artists in Singapore, Xu was friends with Straits-born Chinese who were invested in the political developments of mainland China, among them Lim's son, the war hero Lim Bo Seng.

Xu Beihong. *Portrait of Lim Loh*. 1927. Oil on canvas, 114 × 76 cm. Gift of Lim family in memory of Lim Loh.

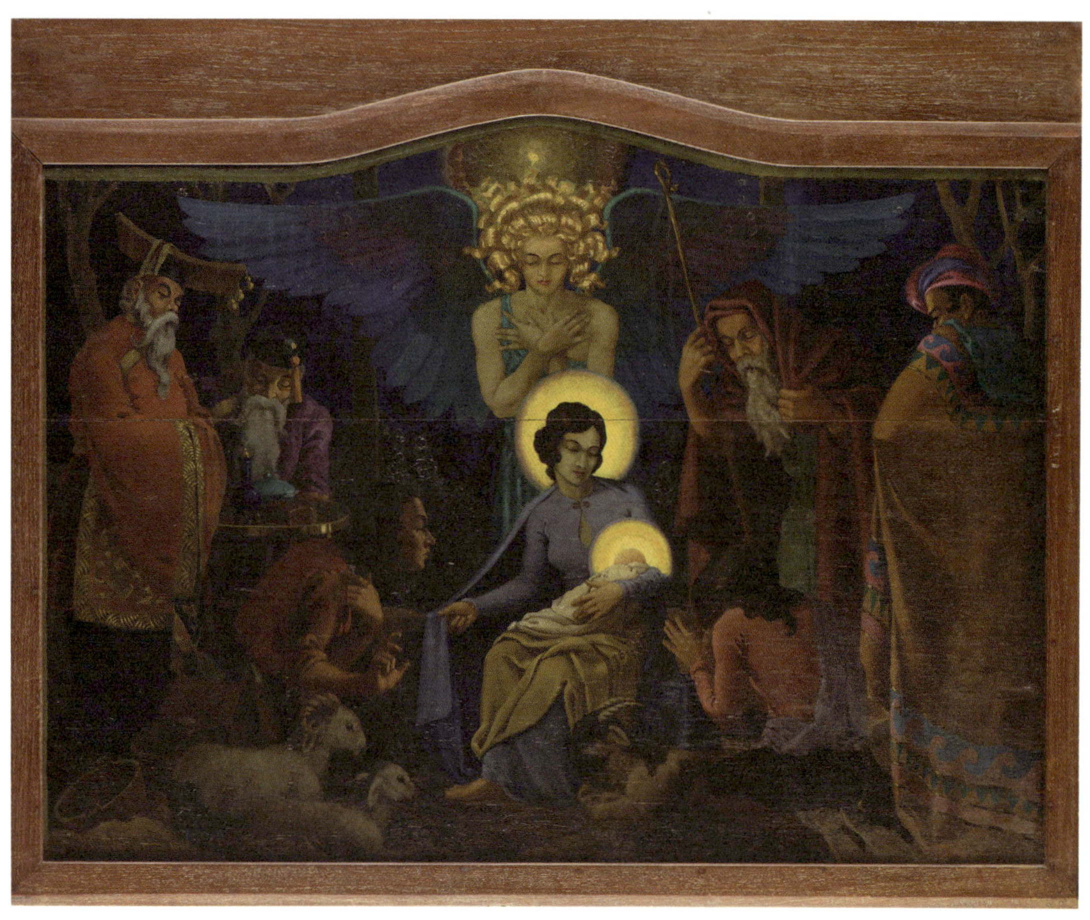

Epiphany is a dreamlike painting produced during the Japanese Occupation of Singapore when the artist Richard Walker was interned in Changi Prison. A complex composition, this painted wooden panel depicts a scene of the birth of Jesus. The characters that typically appear in Nativity scenes are, however, presented differently here—the angel is depicted with a contemporary hairstyle, while one of the Wise Men is shown in traditional Chinese attire.

Richard Walker. *Epiphany*. 1942. Oil on panel, 71 × 98.6 cm. Gift of Rev Dr Moses Tay.

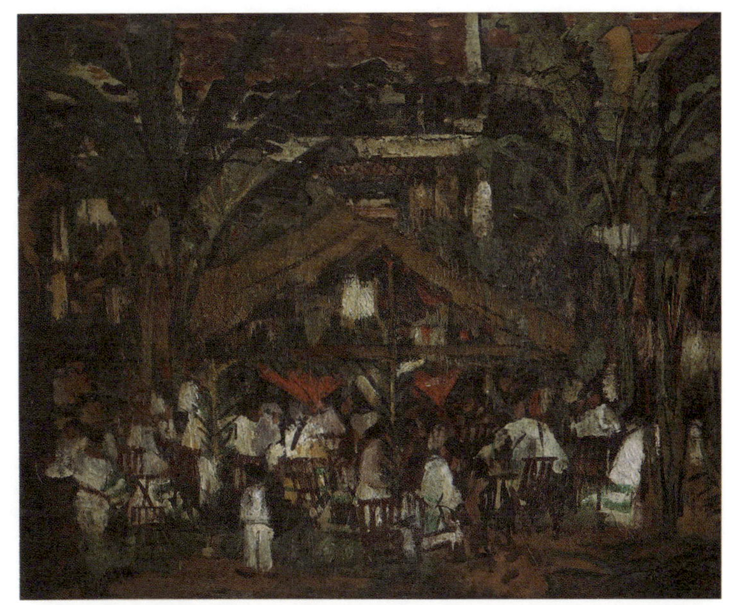

Lim Hak Tai
Malay Wedding
1952
Acrylic on board
70.5 × 96 cm

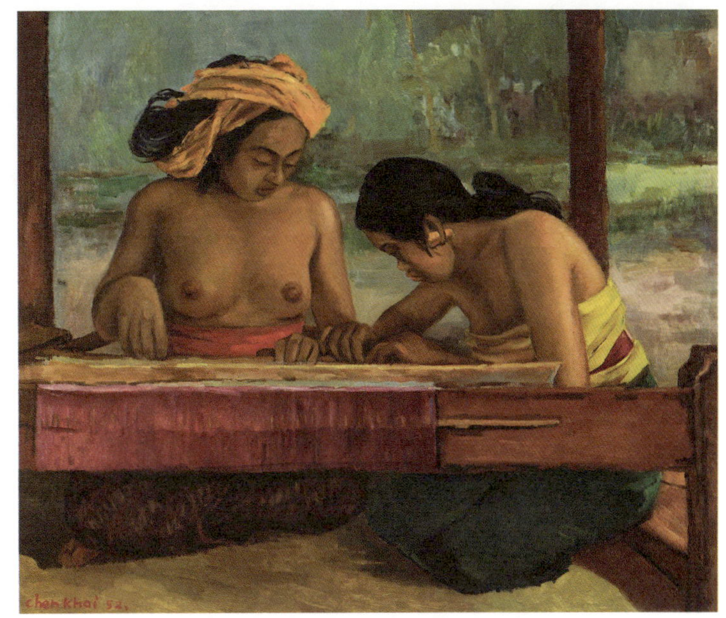

Chen Chong Swee
Weaving
1952
Oil on masonite board
90 × 108 cm
Gift of the family of the late Chen Chong Swee

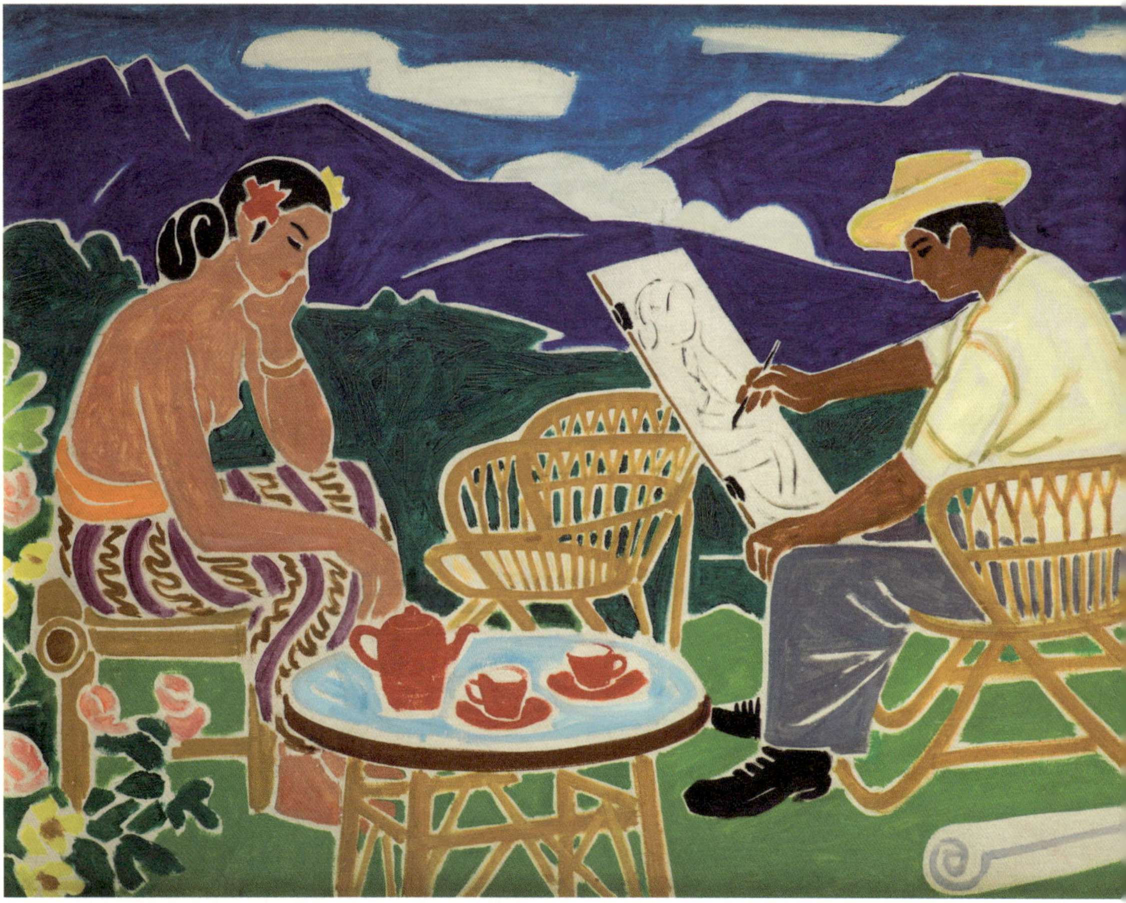

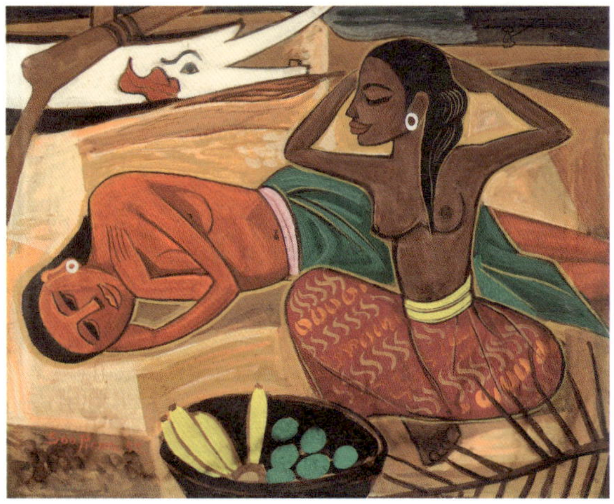

The almond-shaped eyes and slender limbs of these two figures may be described as earlier iterations of Cheong Soo Pieng's distinctive style. Through his many trips around the region, Cheong came into close contact with the peoples and cultures of Southeast Asia. His observations informed his works—the rich, deep colours of this painting, as well as the use of tropical motifs like bananas and palm leaves, is a fitting example.

Cheong Soo Pieng. *Bali Beach*. 1955. Gouache on cardboard laid on masonite, 50 × 63 cm. Bequest of Loke Wan Tho.

Artist and Model features an artist's take on another artist—inspired when he saw fellow artist Chen Wen Hsi at work in Surabaya, Liu Kang sketched the scene, later basing this painting on that sketch. This is one of the earliest paintings that highlights the role of local artists in imagining, reconstructing, and projecting the region. Note, for instance, the way Liu Kang has sublimated the dramatic terrain of Java into blocks of striking colour.

Liu Kang. *Artist and Model.* 1954. Oil on canvas, 84 × 124 cm. Gift of Shell Group of Companies, Singapore.

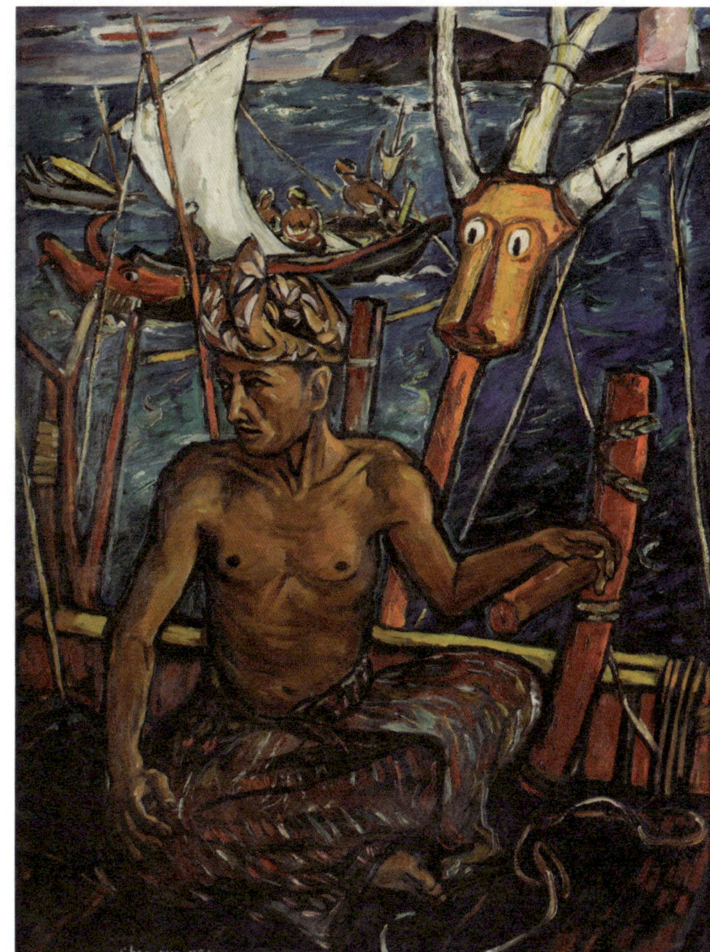

Based on his encounter with a boatman in Bali, The Ferry reveals Chen Wen Hsi's fascination with the island's decorated fishing vessels. Through the use of vivid colours, expressive brushstrokes and dynamic composition, the artist imbues the scene with a sense of movement, recalling the experience of being out at sea. This is one of Chen's significant early works incorporating regional motifs, such as the boatman's headdress and batik *sarong* wrap.

Chen Wen Hsi. *The Ferry.* c. 1952. Oil on canvas, 112.6 × 85.2 cm.

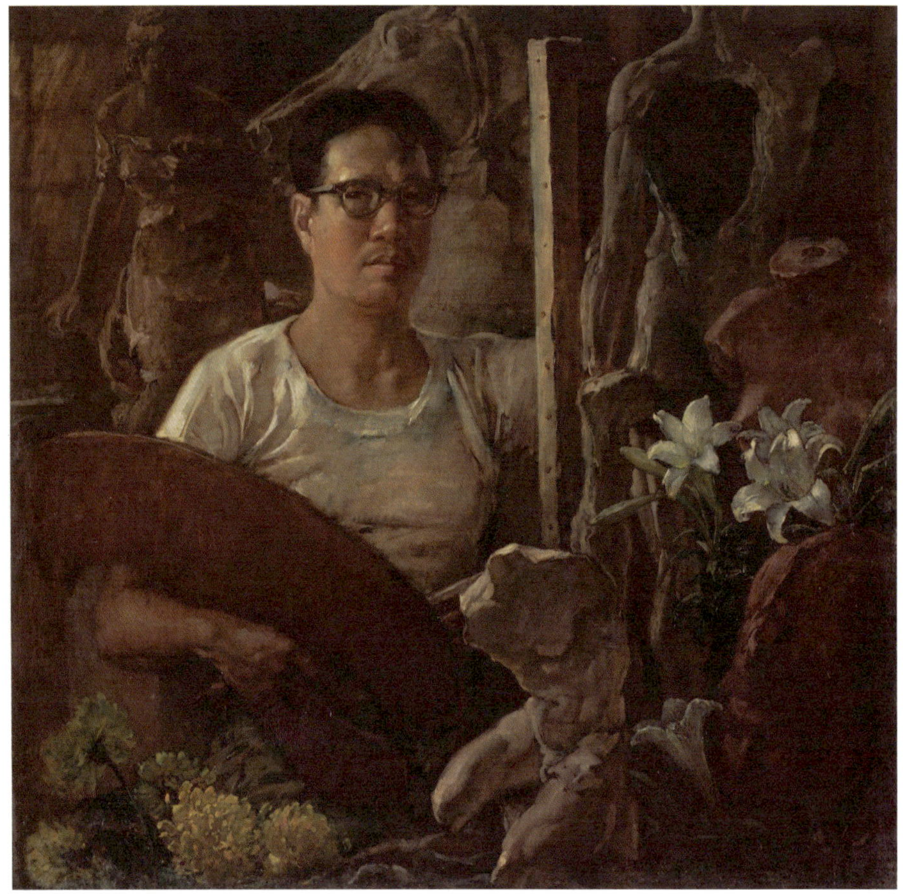

This is a portrait of multiple traditions and cultural influences. The artist, Lee Man Fong, is surrounded by the tools of his profession at the studio. While the busts and plaster casts refer to his familiarity with traditions of European art, there are suggestions of other influences. This may be seen in the chrysanthemums, a common motif in Chinese ink paintings, and Lee's simple attire, which bring to mind the tropics he called home.

Lee Man Fong. *Self Portrait*. 1958. Oil on canvas, 99 × 102 cm. Gift of Mr and Mrs Putra Masagung.

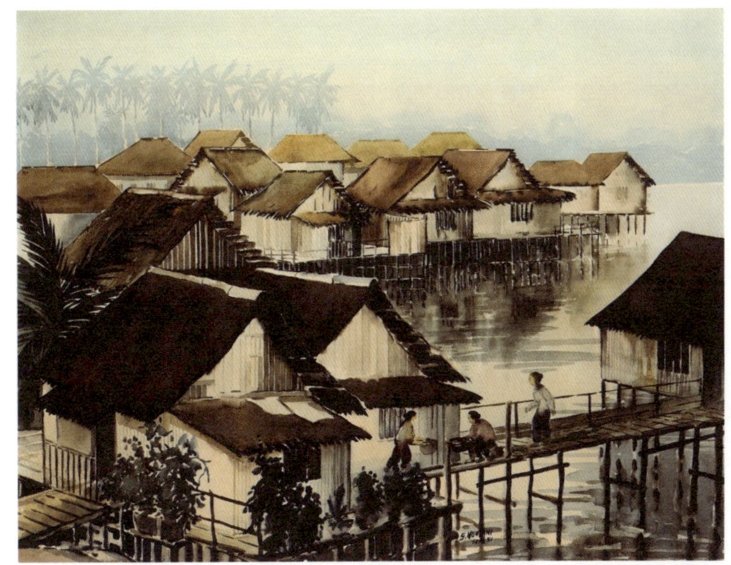

Kampong Kuchan is a fishing village situated off Lorong 3, Geylang. Its inhabitants were believed to be descendants of Orang Laut, which means "sea people" in Malay. Orang Laut, who lived in boats, were already present along the coastline of Singapore in 1819, when Sir Stamford Raffles arrived and established Singapore as a colony; their subsequent relocation to Kampong Kuchan highlights the historical and cultural significance of this site, which no longer exists.

Suri Mohyani. *Kampong Kuchan (Lorong 3, Geylang).* 1951. Watercolour on paper, 45.7 × 60.2 cm.

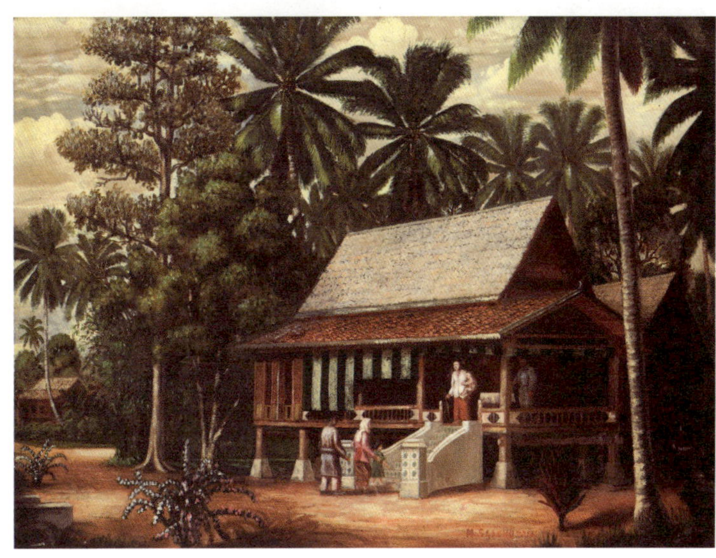

Mohammed Sallehuddin
Malay House, Malacca
c. 1960
Oil on canvas
59 × 79.6 cm

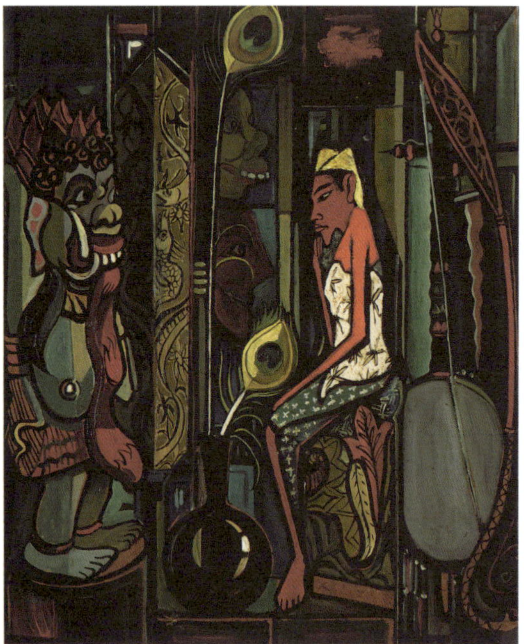

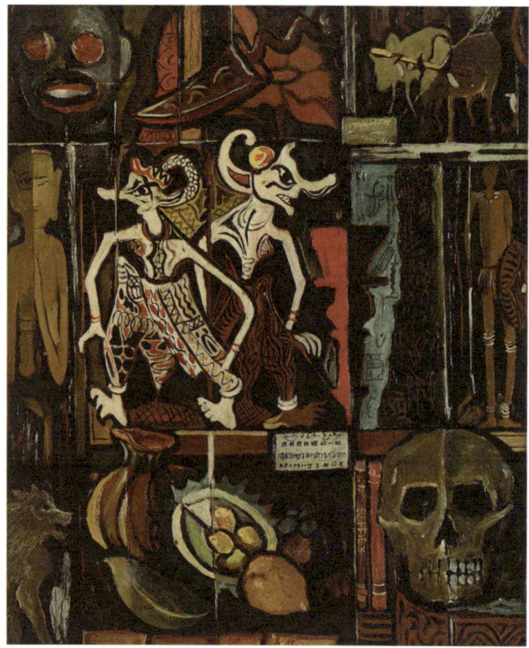

These paintings may have been inspired by artefacts from the region on display at Raffles Museum, which was established by the colonial authorities in 1874 for scientific and anthropological research. Lim Mu Hue was known for his woodcut prints, echoes of which reverberate in the defined lines and bold colours of these two works.

LEFT Lim Mu Hue. *Within the Museum I*. 1957. Oil on masonite board, 58 × 49 cm.
RIGHT Lim Mu Hue. *Within the Museum II*. 1957. Oil on masonite board, 59.4 × 49.2 cm.

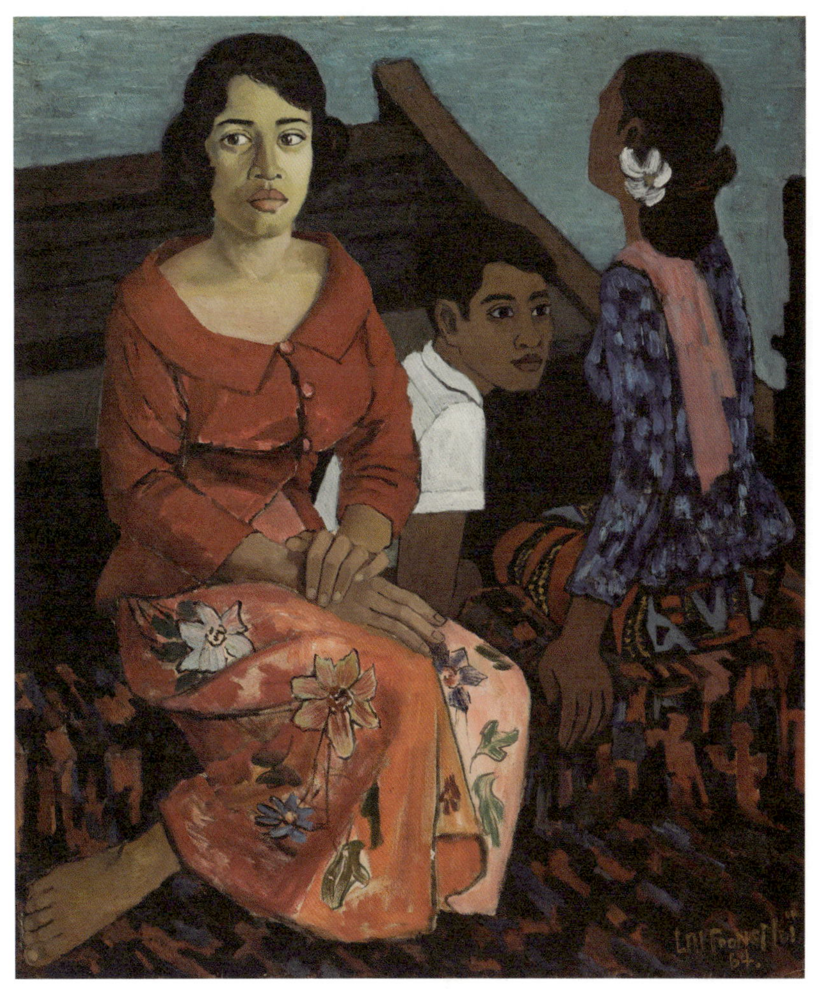

Lai Foong Moi
Home Coming
1964
Oil on canvas
77 × 65 cm
Collection of Singapore Airlines Limited

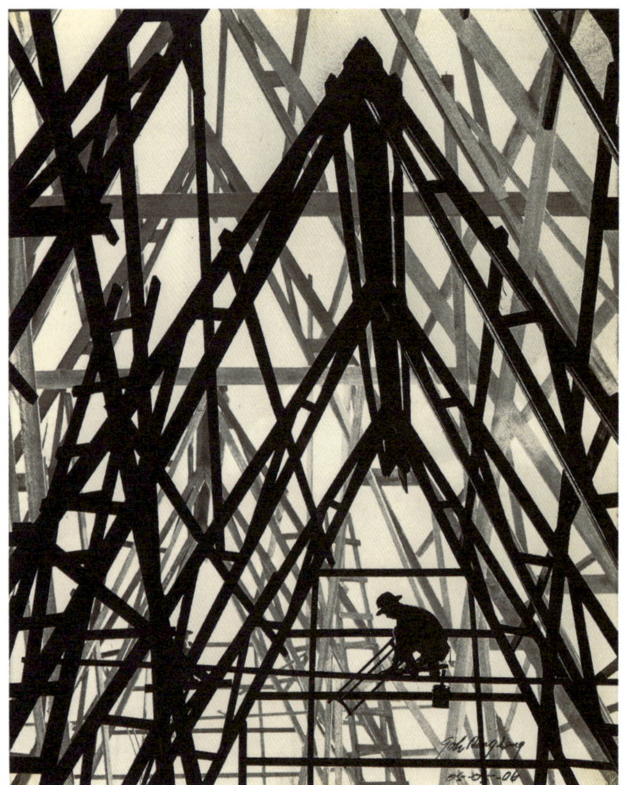

This striking photograph was created by Wu Peng Seng in 1958, when he chanced upon the construction of a temporary exhibition hall at the Paya Lebar Airport. A solitary figure is shown at work, his small silhouette framed by towering triangular roof trusses that provide a sense of depth. Bold lines and extreme tonal contrast further imbue the image with a graphic and modern sensibility.

Wu Peng Seng. *Construction*. 1958. Gelatin silver print, 49.5 × 40 cm.

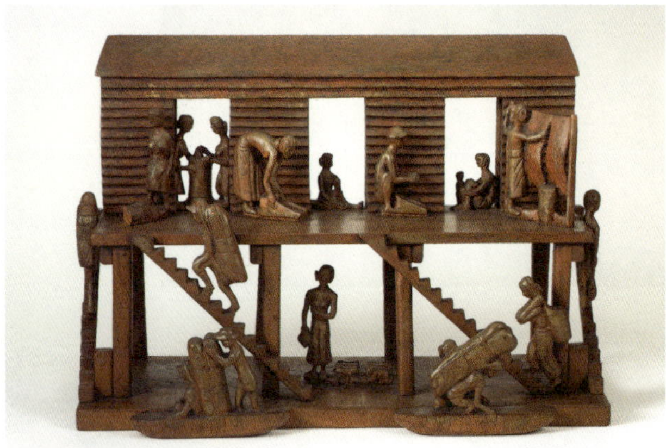

Shui Tit Sing
Longhouse
1980
Teak
47 × 69 × 29 cm

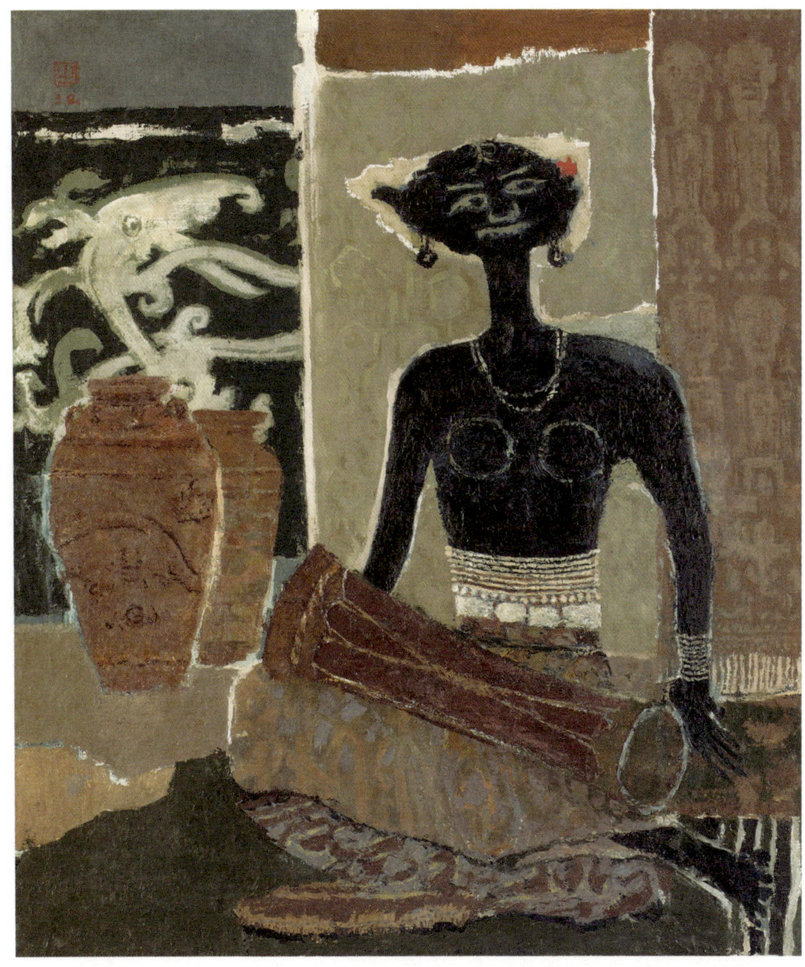

An accomplished calligrapher, Yeh Chi Wei combined his interest in archaic Chinese inscriptions with influences from Southeast Asian figurative sculptures and textiles to develop his own visual language. This painting was inspired by one of Yeh's regional field trips made as a member of the Ten Men Art Group, which was active in the 1960s.

Yeh Chi Wei. *Drummer*. 1965. Oil on canvas, 104.5 × 91.5 cm.

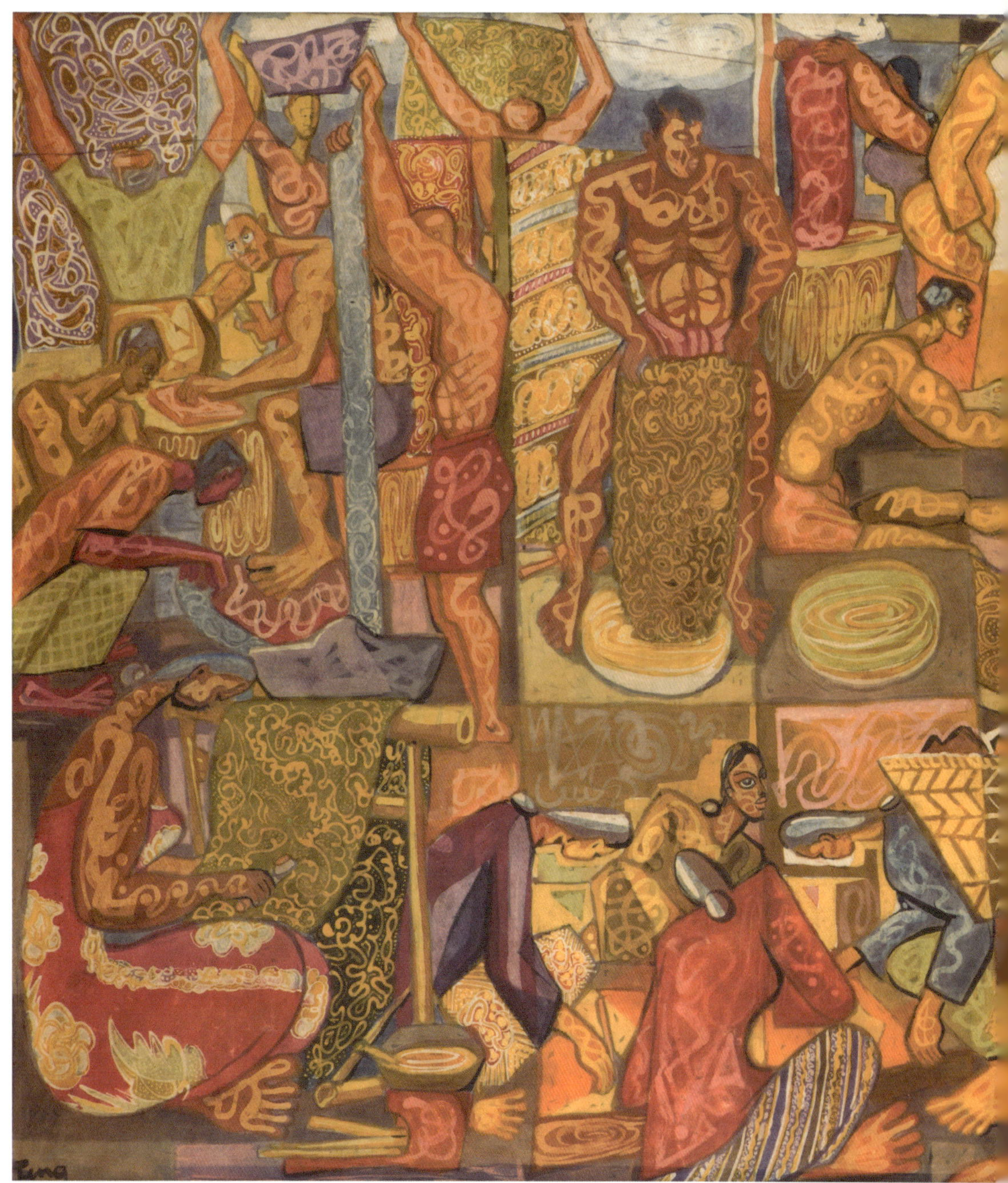

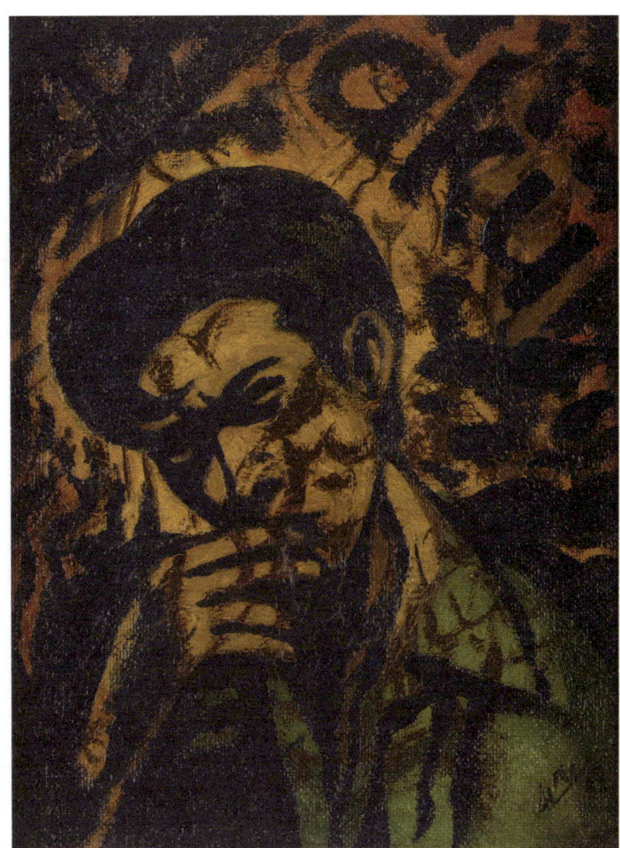

This work is an homage to Indonesian poet Chairil Anwar, whose poetry Malaysian artist Latiff Mohidin encountered while studying in Singapore. *Aku*, which stands for "I" in Malay, is also the title of Anwar's most celebrated poem; written in 1943 while Indonesia was in the throes of the Japanese Occupation, it has been read as an exhortation to take charge of one's environment and to be a critical agent in imagining one's nation.

Latiff Mohidin. *Aku*. 1958. Oil on board, 40 × 30 cm.

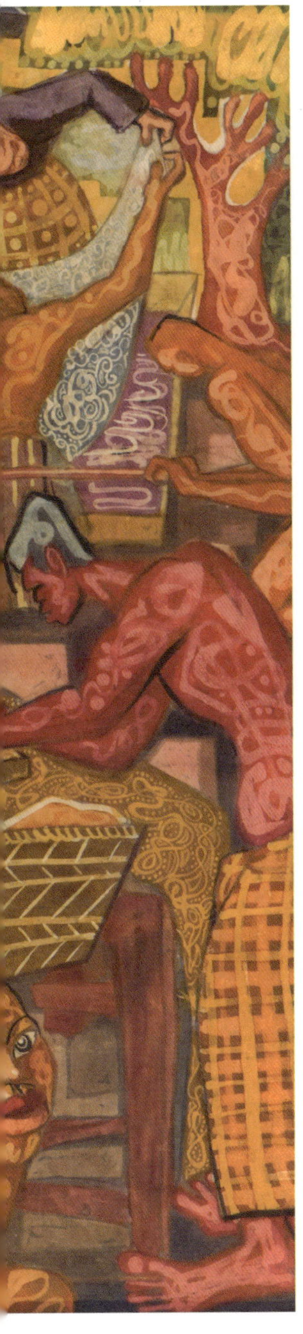

In the 1950s, Chuah Thean Teng was the first artist in Malaya to transform batik—a traditional dyeing technique used to adorn textiles with decorative folk and religious symbols—into a medium of fine art. Chuah's paintings of this period, like those of his contemporaries, often present a romanticised view of Malayan life.

Chuah Thean Teng. *Sarong-Making Shop*. c. 1957. Batik, 73.3 × 88 cm.

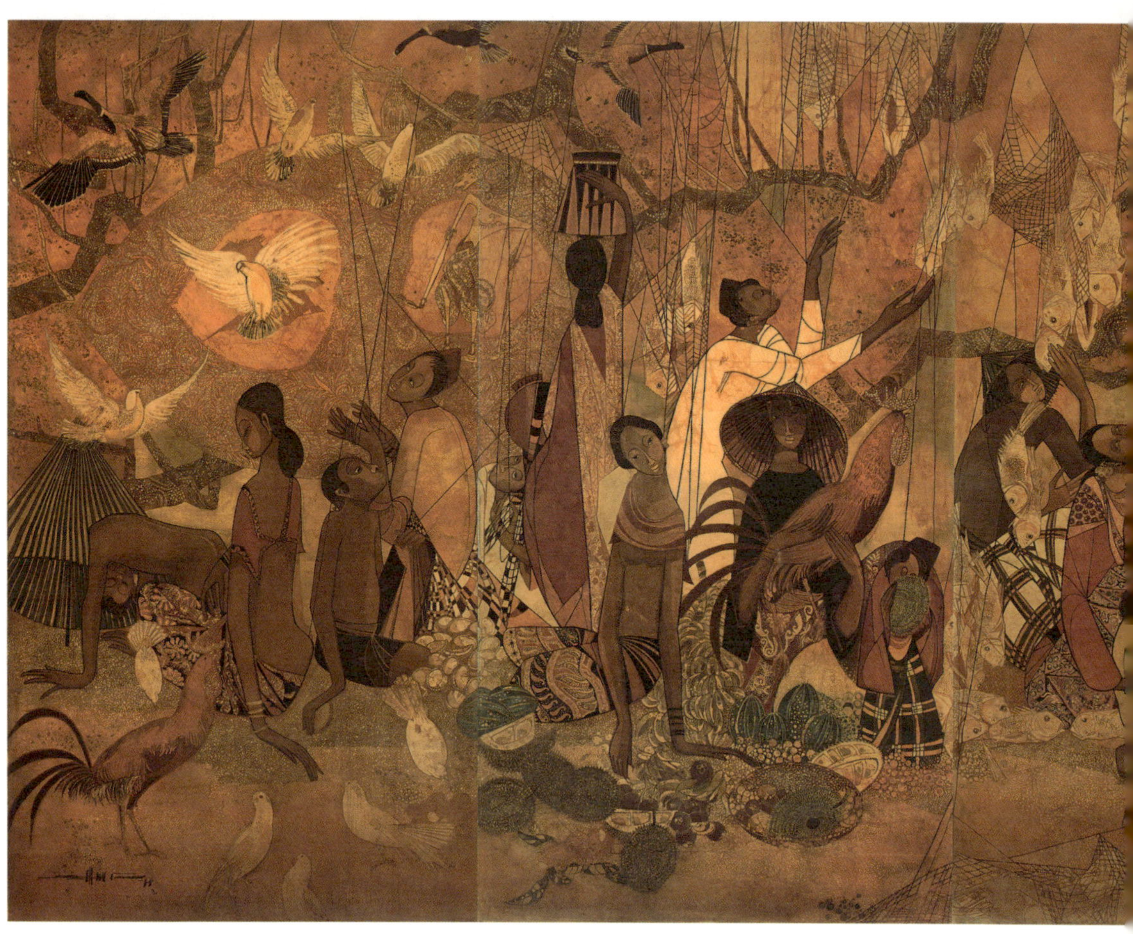

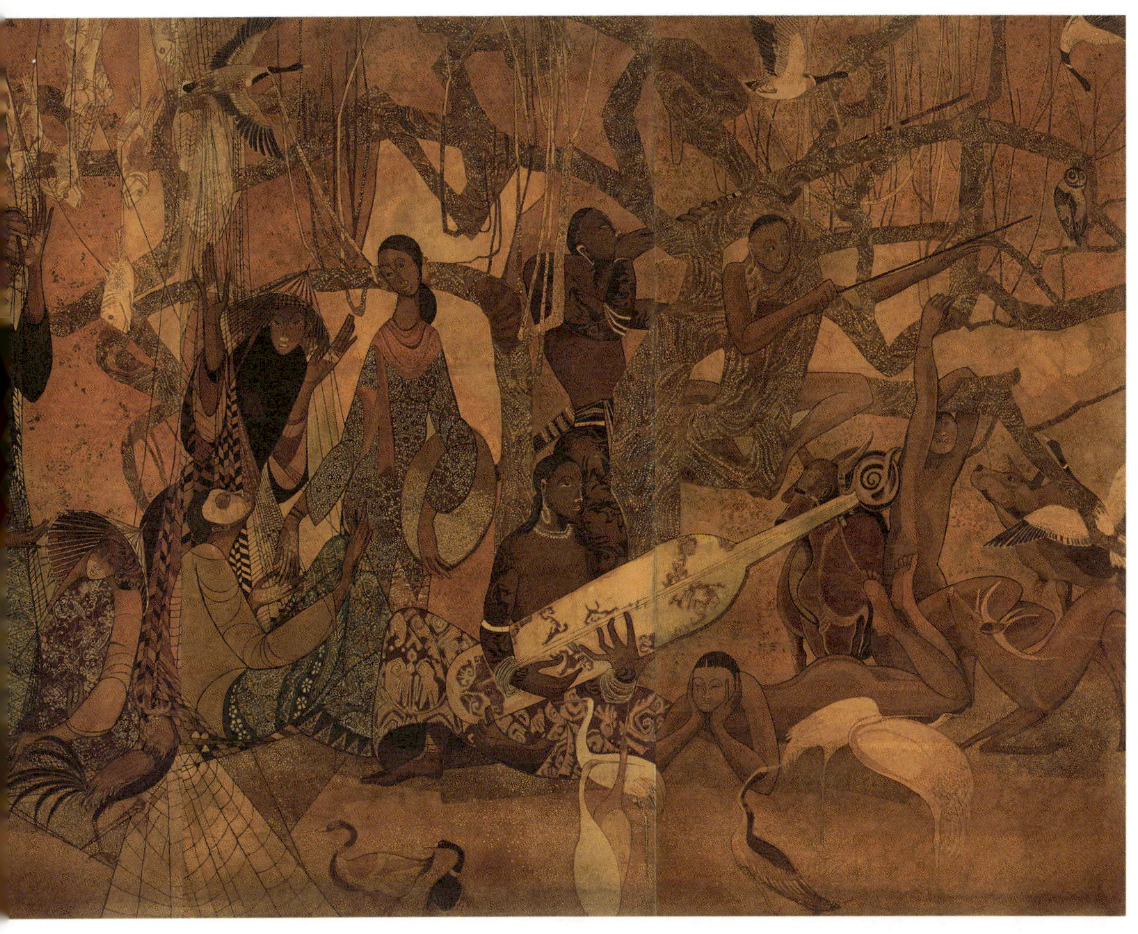

Scenes of salted fish hanging out to dry, indigenous hunters in pursuit of their prey, and womenfolk sitting amid bountiful harvests of land and sea form an idyllic narrative of rural Malaya. Seah Kim Joo originally created this mural for the foyer of the now defunct Hotel Malaysia, one of the grandest hotels in Singapore then. His graceful rendition of the human figures, interwoven in this elaborate composition, display his virtuosity in batik.

Seah Kim Joo. *Untitled* (*Malayan Life*). 1968. Batik, 256 × 694 cm. LASALLE College of the Arts Collection, Institute of Contemporary Arts Singapore. Acquired 1996.

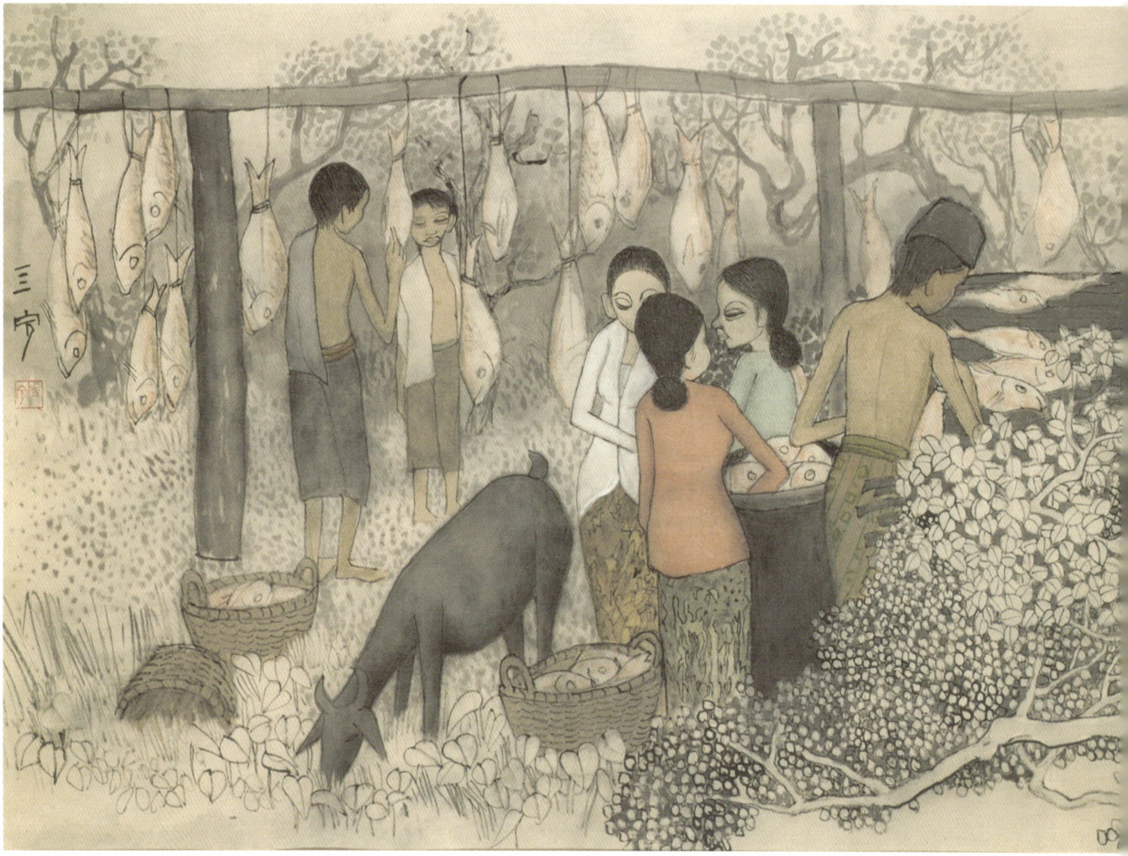

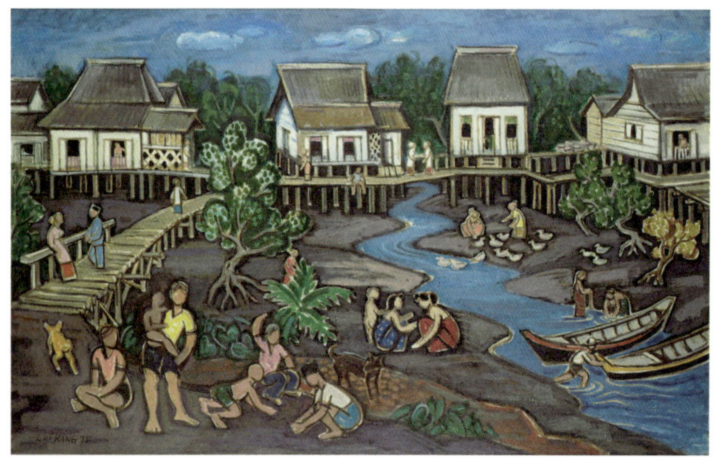

Liu Kang's painting resembles the unfurling story of a Chinese handscroll, where carefully positioned subjects lead the eye of the viewer across the work. The arching boardwalk and sinuous river unite various figures in the painting, lending it a coherence that attests to the artist's compositional skills.

Liu Kang. *Life by the River.* 1975. Oil on canvas, 126 × 203 cm. Gift of Liu Kang.

Scenes of salted fish drying in the sun were common from the 1940s to the 1960s, particularly along the coast of Singapore and Malaya. In his depiction of this everyday scene, Cheong Soo Pieng skillfully employs both Chinese ink painting techniques and Western fixed-point perspective. Like many of his contemporaries, Cheong constantly sought to interpret Southeast Asian landscapes in new ways. This iconic painting is featured on the back of Singapore's $50 banknote.

Cheong Soo Pieng. *Drying Salted Fish*. 1978. Chinese ink and watercolour on cloth, 55.5 × 88.5 cm. Gift of Trans Island Bus Services Ltd.

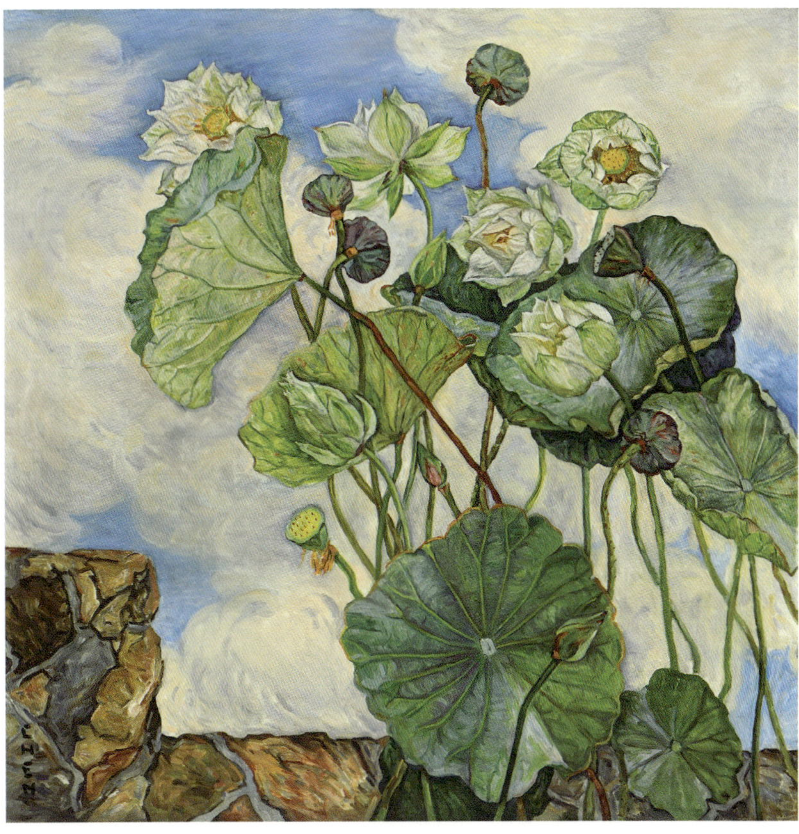

Like the French Impressionists she encountered as an art student, Georgette Chen loved working outdoors to capture the fleeting effects of natural light. This painting was produced similarly, as Chen's diary entry records: "For ten days, the day began for me at 7 a.m. and ended at 6 p.m. Under my painting sun shade, I feasted on these delicate white and pink beauties." This is a classic example of a Nanyang artist using Western pictorial techniques to depict a local subject.

Georgette Chen. *Lotus in a Breeze*. c. 1970. Oil on canvas, 81 × 81 cm. Gift of Lee Foundation.

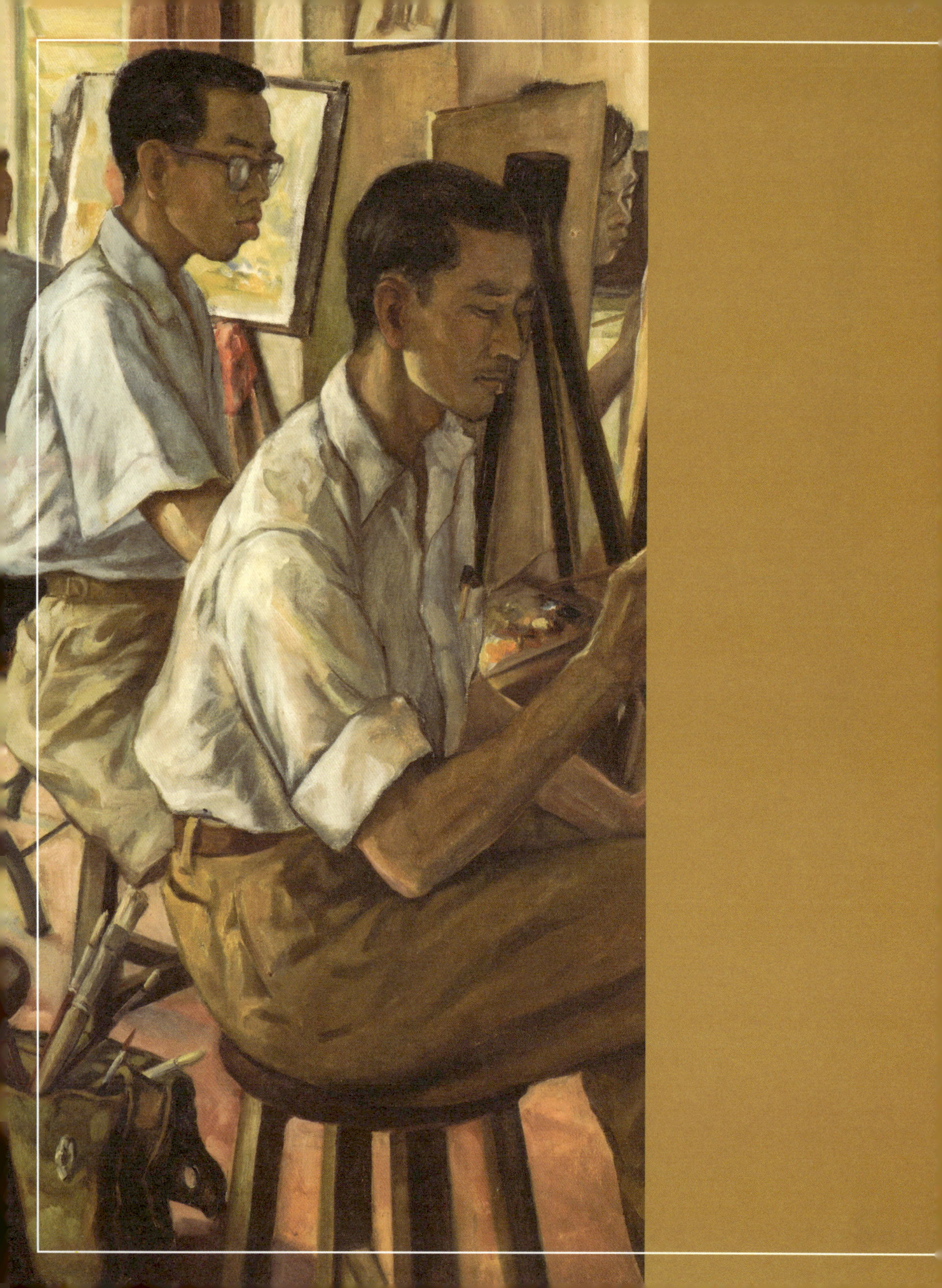

Real Concerns

"Art belongs to the people—it is the public, and should serve the public," declared a group of Chinese middle school students in Singapore who had united for an exhibition in 1956.

The belief that art had the power to effect social change was shared by many artists who experienced the raging anti-colonial movements in Malaya after World War II. In light of the tumultuous events of the 1950s, it became apparent for many that representing an idyllic Nanyang was no longer sufficient; art had to expose prevailing social conditions and portray the marginalised with empathy. As Singapore moved toward self-governance, issues of identity also came to the fore, as is silently evident in the stoic self-portraits and tense portraits of family and friends created by artists. Even as art reflected the realities of social upheaval, it also had to be aspirational, holding the promise of independence and nationhood.

After Singapore gained independence in 1965, art came to engage with the effects of modernisation. Artists looked both forward and back, seeking to capture the many facades of Singapore's rapidly-changing landscape. Scenes of Singapore's industrialisation stand next to elegiac paintings depicting places of old and past ways of life; an example of the latter are scenes of the Singapore River in watercolour, a medium that grew in prominence in this period.

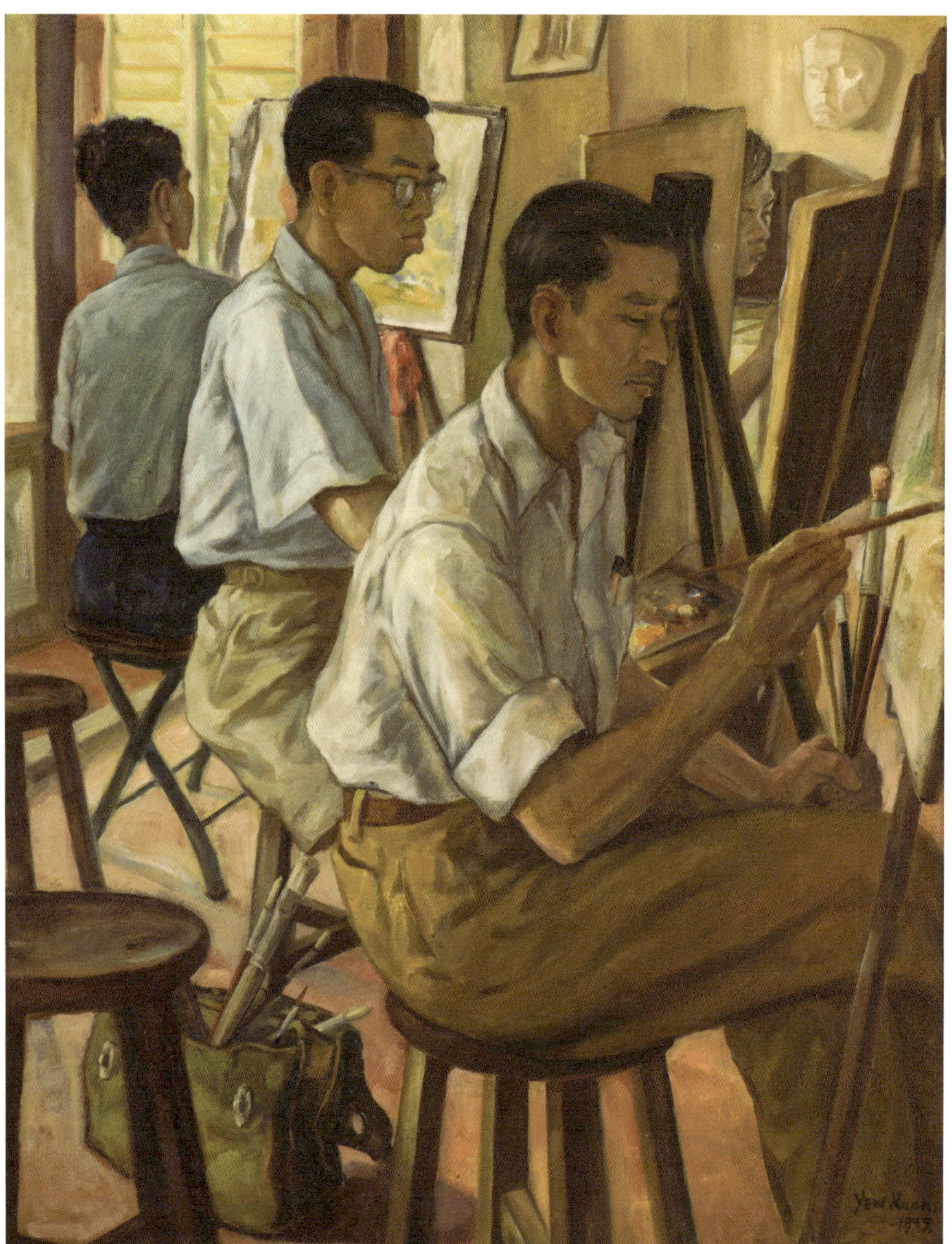

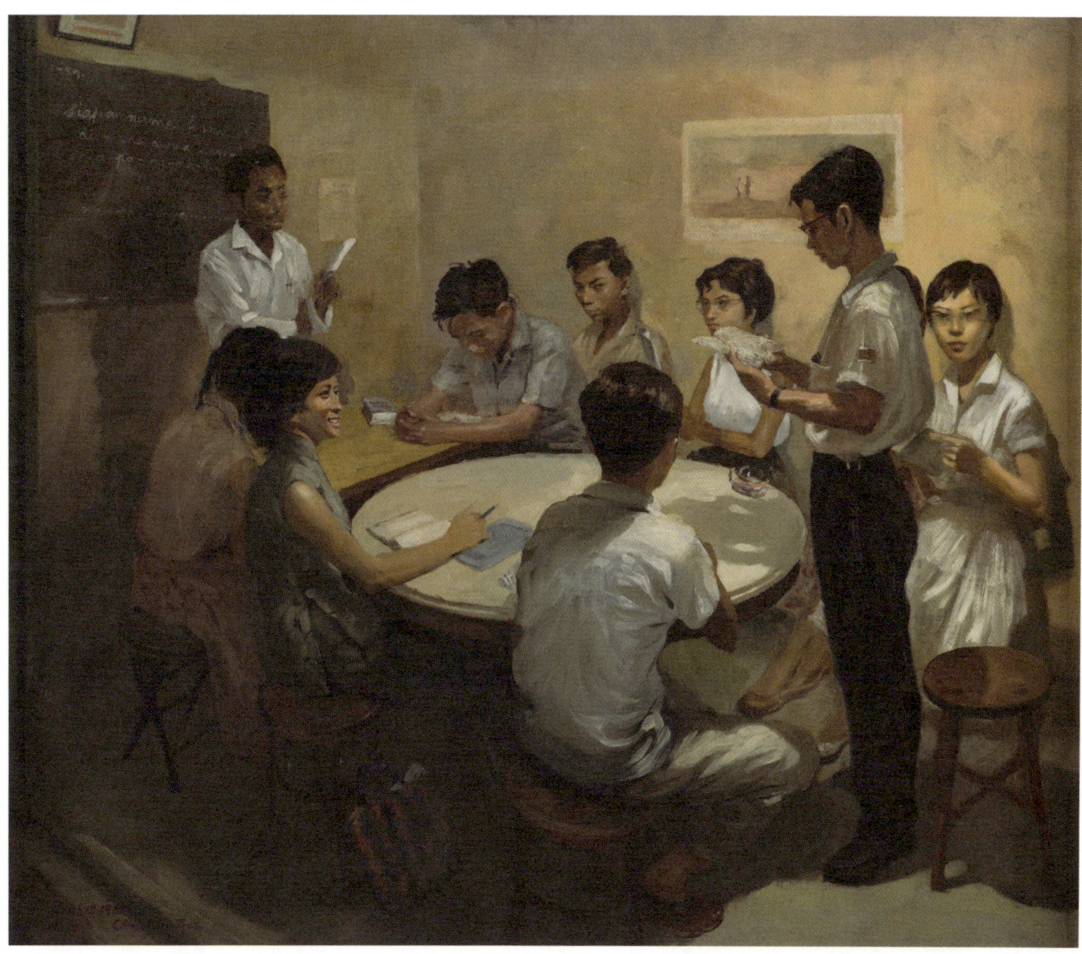

Shortly after Singapore gained partial self-governance in 1955, Malay was made the national language to help bolster the identity of a nation seeking full independence. On the chalkboard are the phrases *Siapa nama kamu?* (What is your name?) and *Di mana awak tinggal?* (Where do you live?), questions that suggest a growing consciousness of national identity among Singaporeans at the time.

Chua Mia Tee. *National Language Class*. 1959. Oil on canvas, 112 × 153 cm.

OPPOSITE PAGE

Enclosed and intimate, this work depicts a painting class in session. The artist Lim Yew Kuan has paid considerable attention to the linear contours of the human figures, as well as objects like the easels and stools, therein revealing an interest in delineating forms. In this way Painting Class leads us to consider not just what is depicted, but how it is depicted—the act of painting itself.

Lim Yew Kuan. *Painting Class*. 1957. Oil on canvas, 83 × 65 cm.

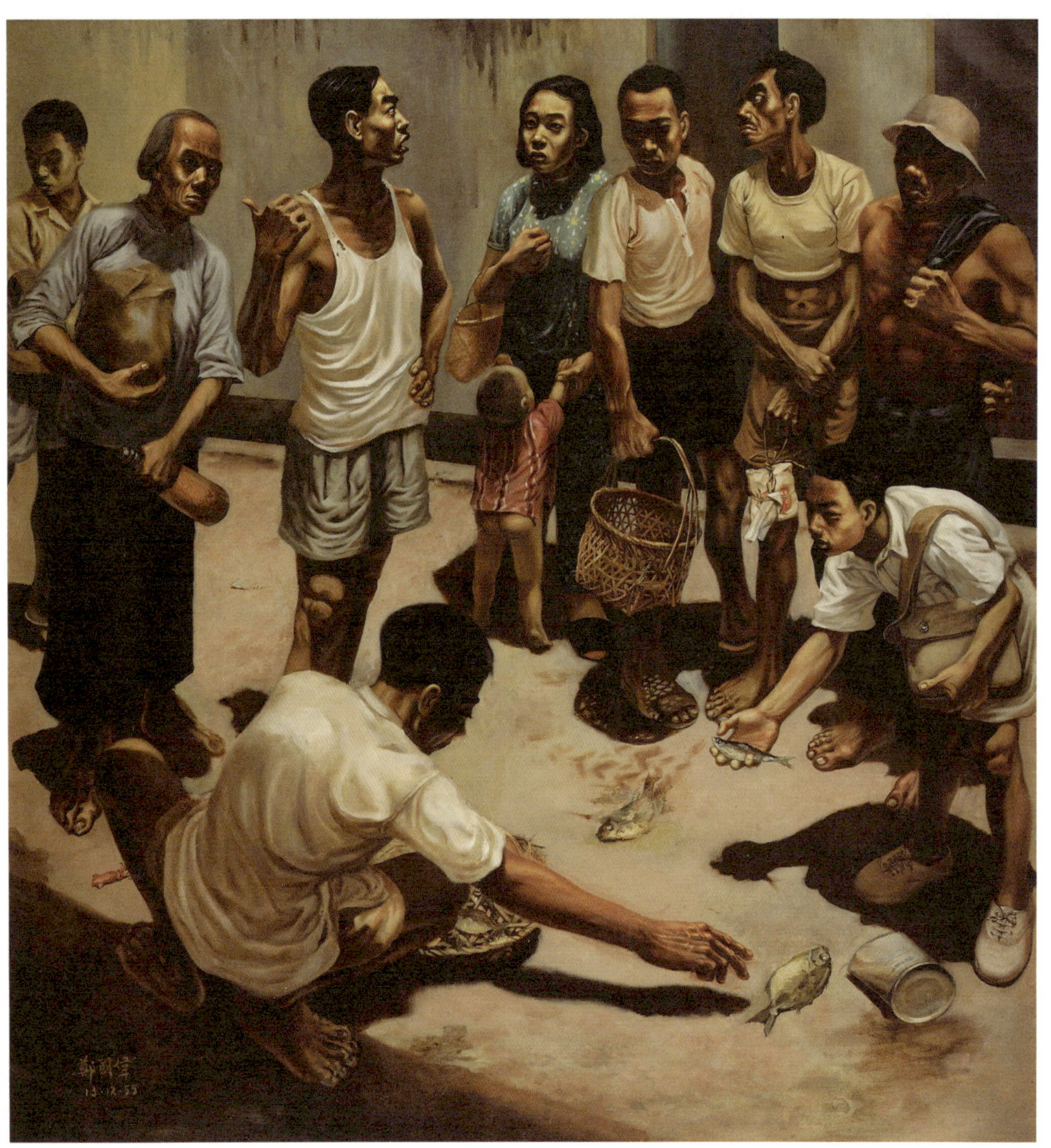

Tay Kok Wee
Picking
1955
Oil on canvas
103.5 × 98 cm

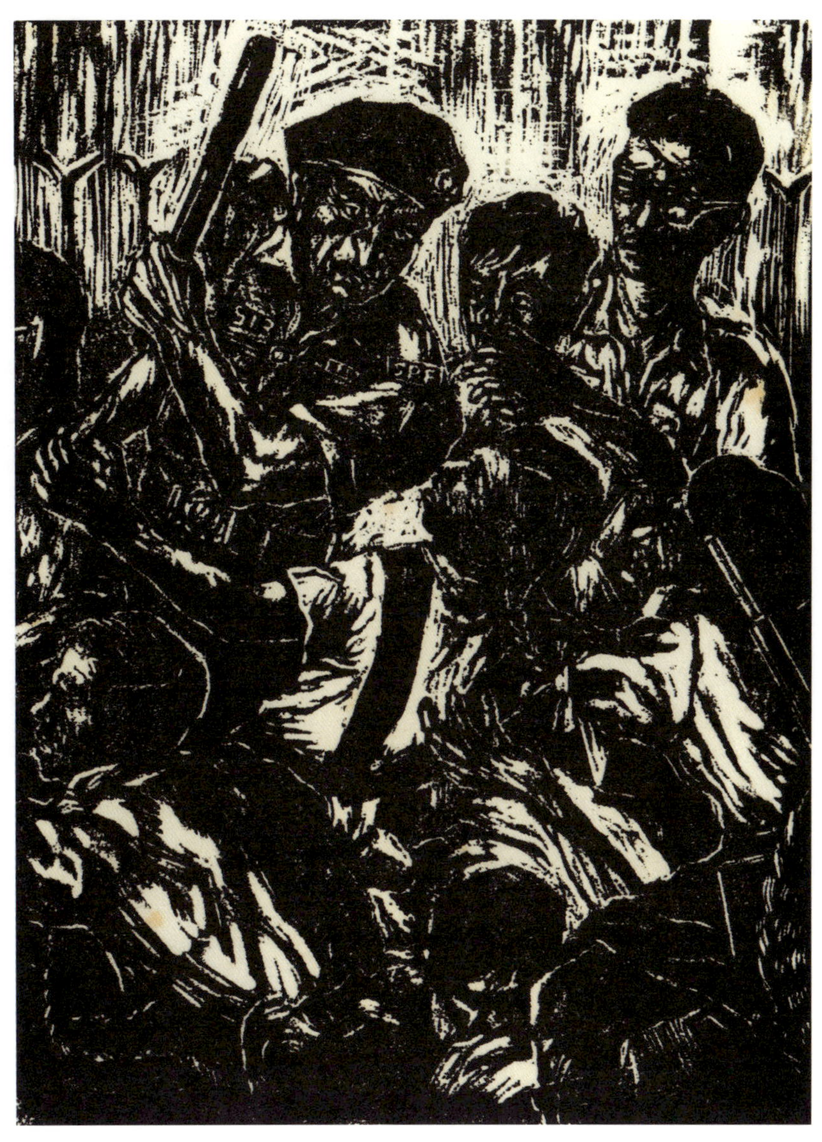

Choo Keng Kwang
Incident 513
1954
Woodblock print on paper
20.5 × 15.5 cm

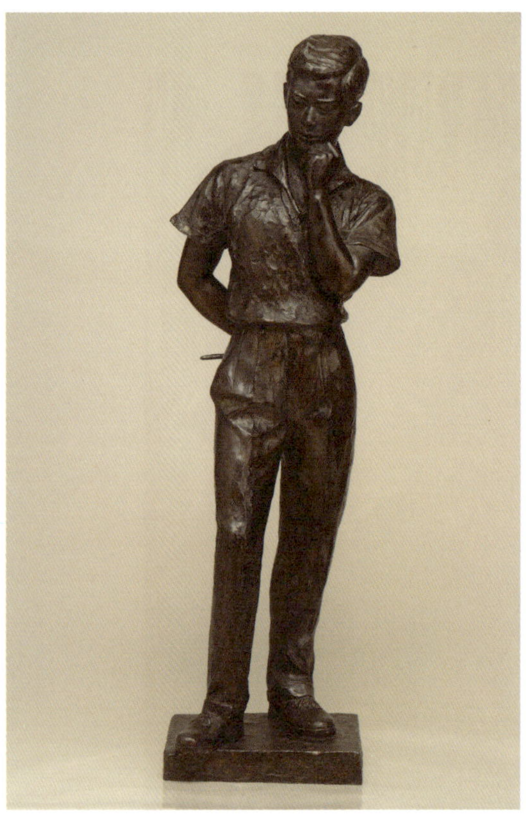

Lee Boon Wang
Before the Moment of Painting
1959
Plaster of Paris
81.8 × 22.5 × 23 cm

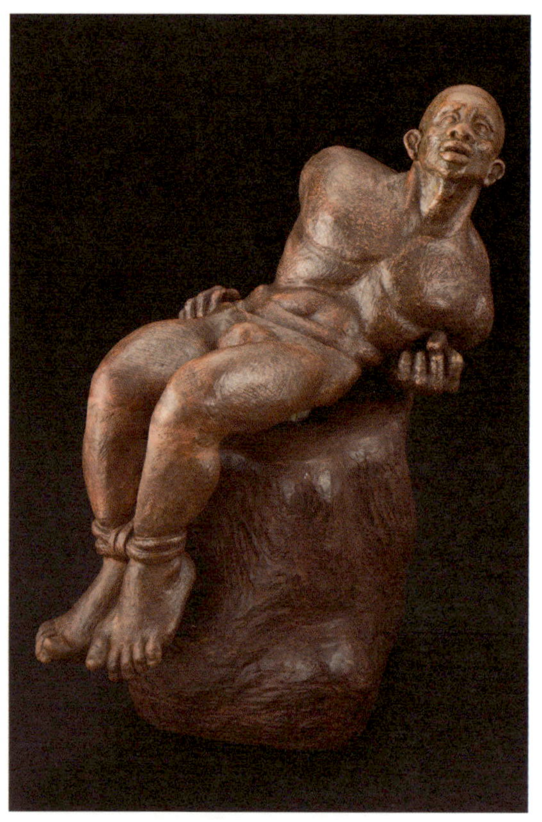

Ng Eng Teng
Bondage
1960
Clay and plaster
40.5 × 26 × 33.5 cm
Gift of Pamela Hickley

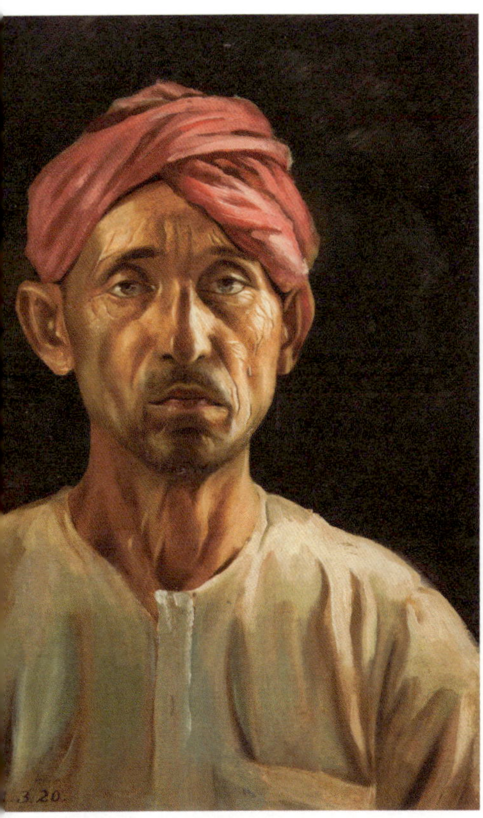

This portrait reveals the artist's meticulous attention in capturing the appearance of his sitter. The farmer's desolate expression, as well as his weathered visage and sinewy frame, hint at the harsh realities of his social and economic condition.

Lee Boon Wang. *Potong Pasir Dairy Farmer.* 1958. Oil on canvas, 54 × 43 cm.

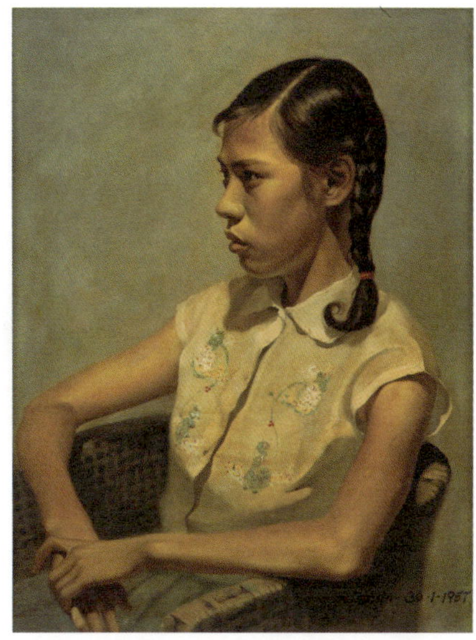

Chua Mia Tee. *Portrait of Lee Boon Ngan.* 1957. Oil on canvas, 65 × 51 cm.

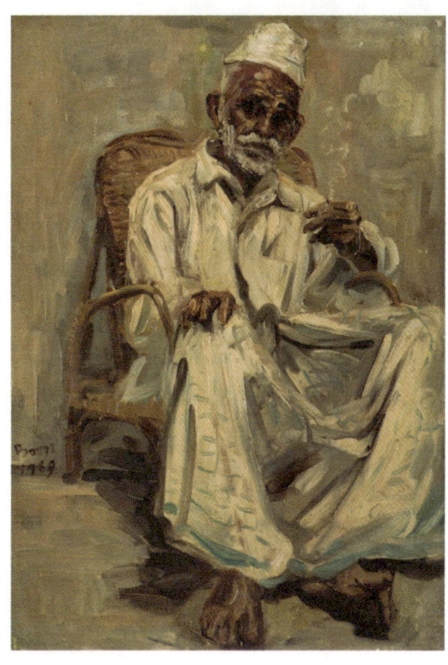

Tay Boon Pin. *Teh Tarik Seller.* 1969. Oil on canvas, 64 × 46 cm.

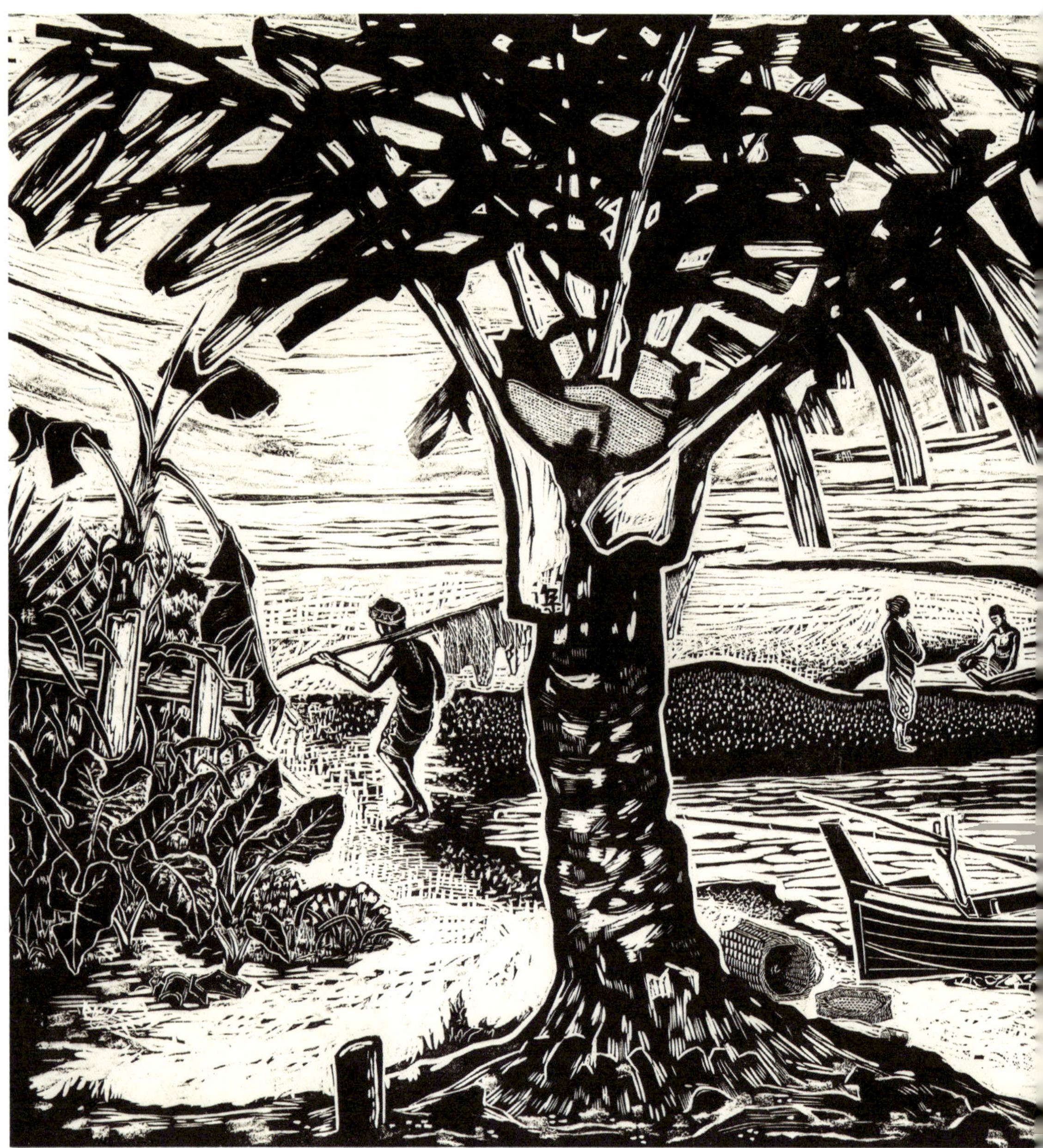

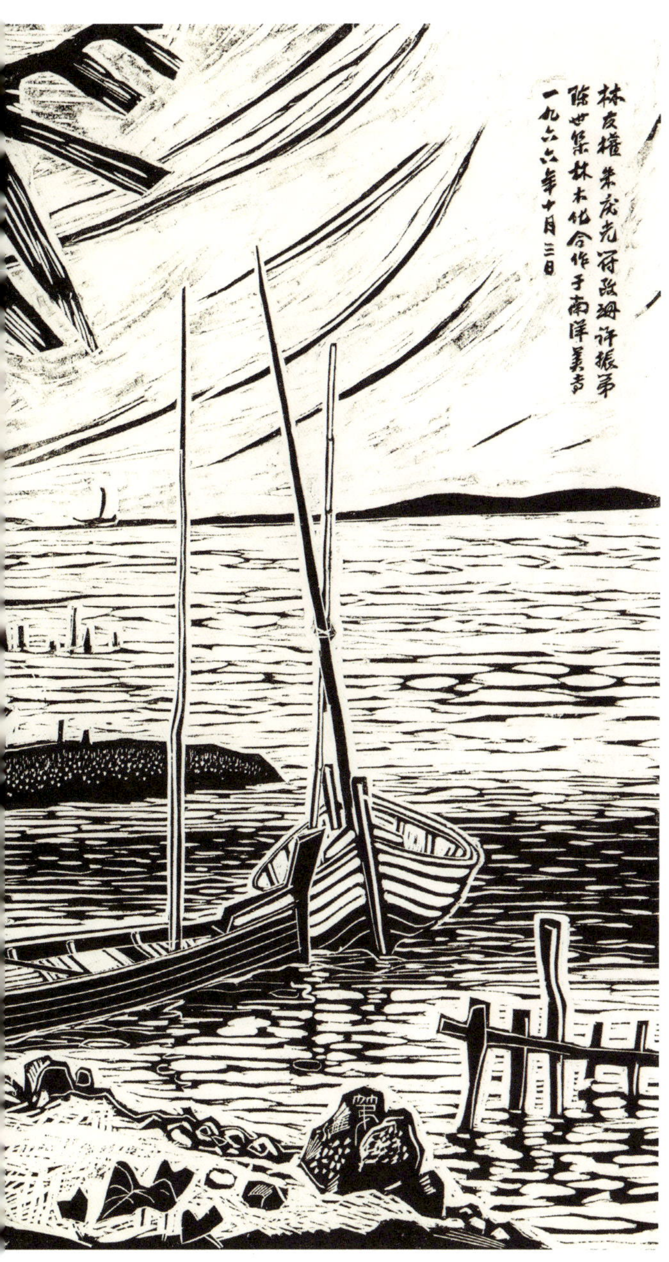

Seascape is the result of a memorable collaboration between six artists. Each of them carved a portion of the woodblock separately, without any preliminary plans for its composition. This work was produced for Singapore's first exhibition of woodblock prints in 1966, a year after Singapore witnessed political turmoil and, eventually, independence. Its tranquillity contrasts with the artists' earlier woodblock prints, which tended to carry socio-political undertones.

Choo Keng Kwang, Foo Chee San, Lim Mu Hue, Lim Yew Kuan, See Cheen Tee, Tan Tee Chie. *Seascape*. 1966. Woodblock print on paper, 77 × 122 cm. Gift of 6-Men Woodcut Artists, Choo Keng Kwang, Foo Chee San, Lim Mu Hue, Lim Yew Kuan, See Cheen Tee and Tan Tee Chie.

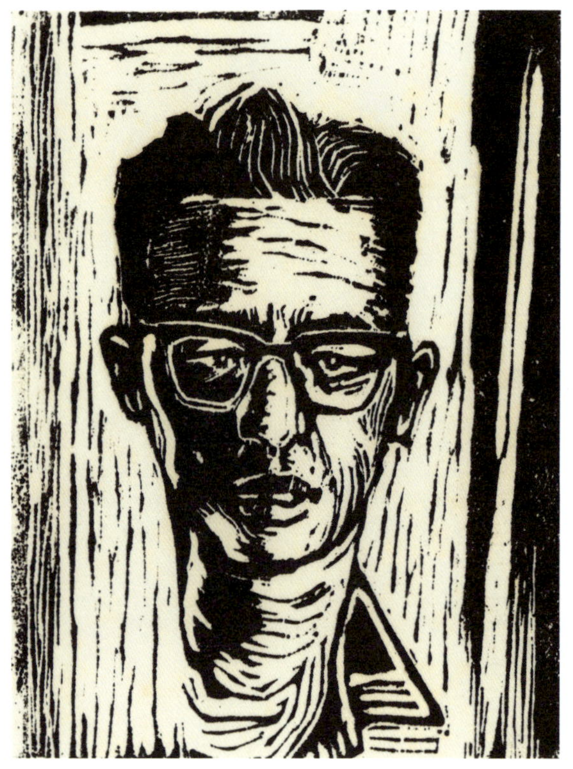

Choo Keng Kwang
Self Portrait
1960
Woodblock print on paper
17 × 12 cm

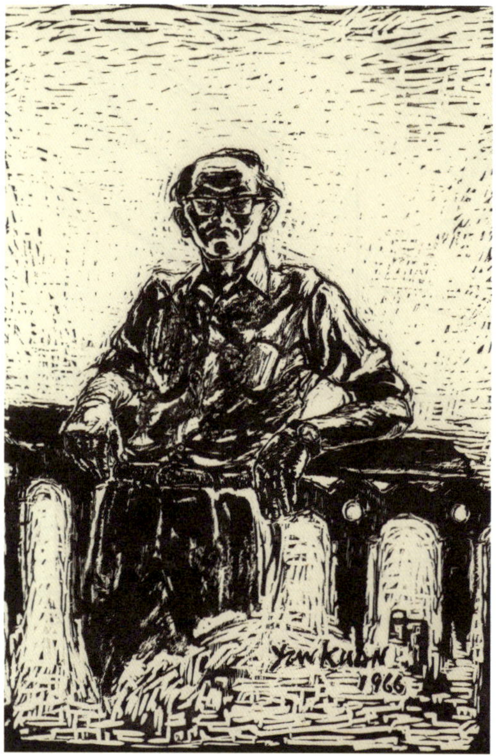

Lim Yew Kuan
Mr Foo Chee San
1966
Woodblock print on paper
55.5 × 37.5 cm

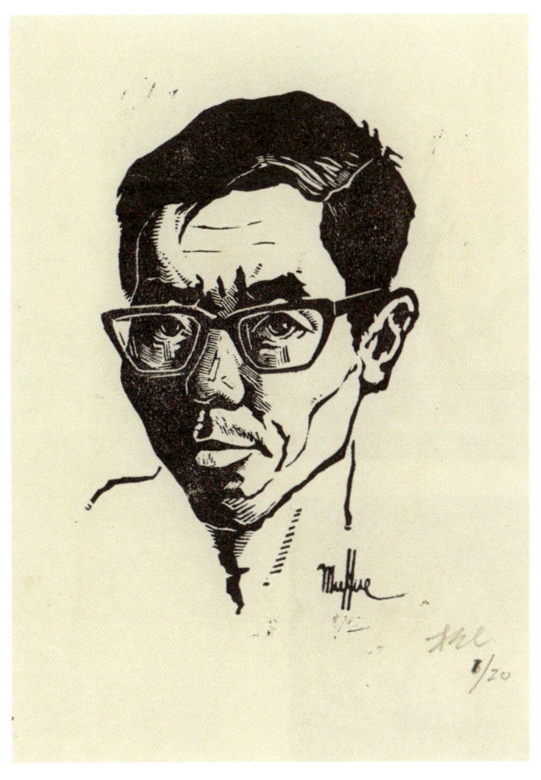

Lim Mu Hue
Self Portrait
1960s
Woodblock print on paper
20.9 × 16.6 cm
Collection of Fukuoka Asian Art Museum

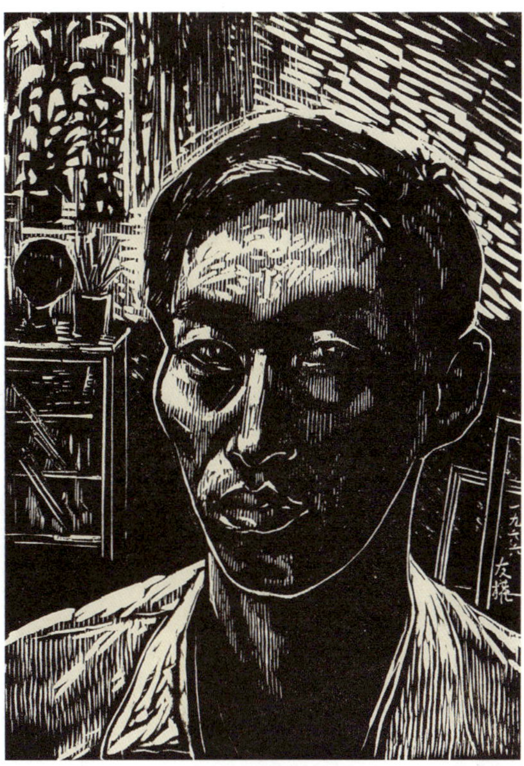

Lim Yew Kuan
Self Portrait II
1966
Woodblock print on paper
20.5 × 15 cm

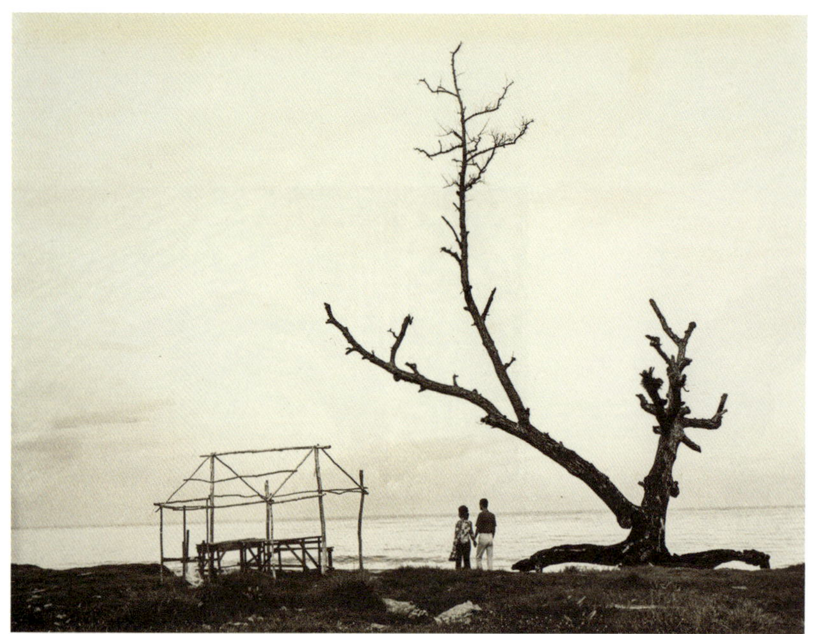

Chua Tiag Ming
Solitude
c. 1960–1970
Photograph
22.6 × 29.6 cm

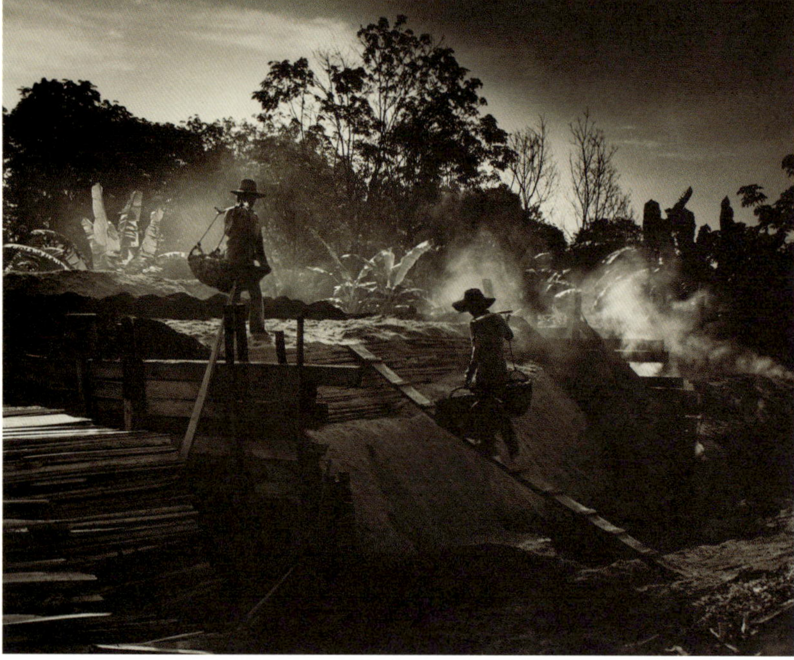

Chua Tiag Ming
Title not known
c. 1960–1970
Photograph
40 × 49 cm

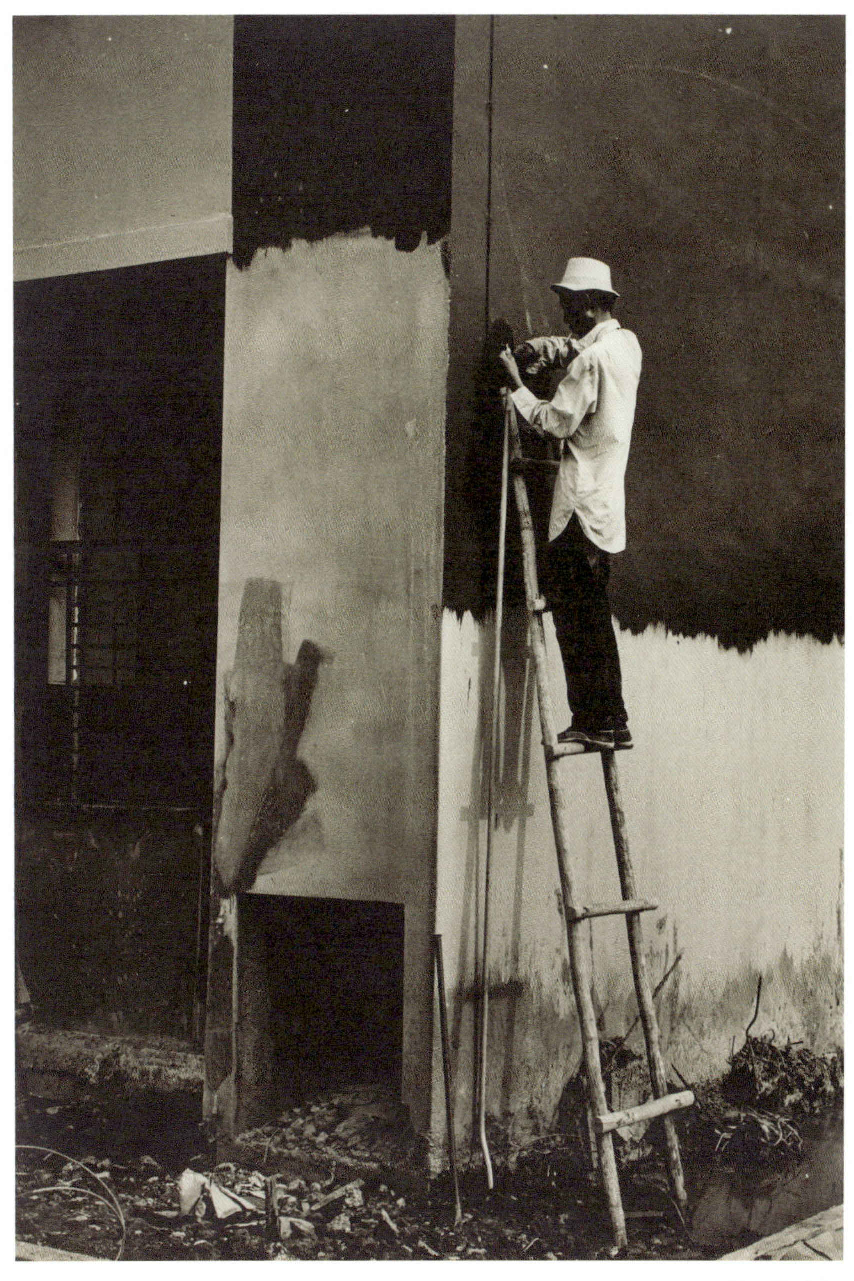

Chua Tiag Ming
Modern Art
c. 1960–1970
Photograph
45 × 31 cm

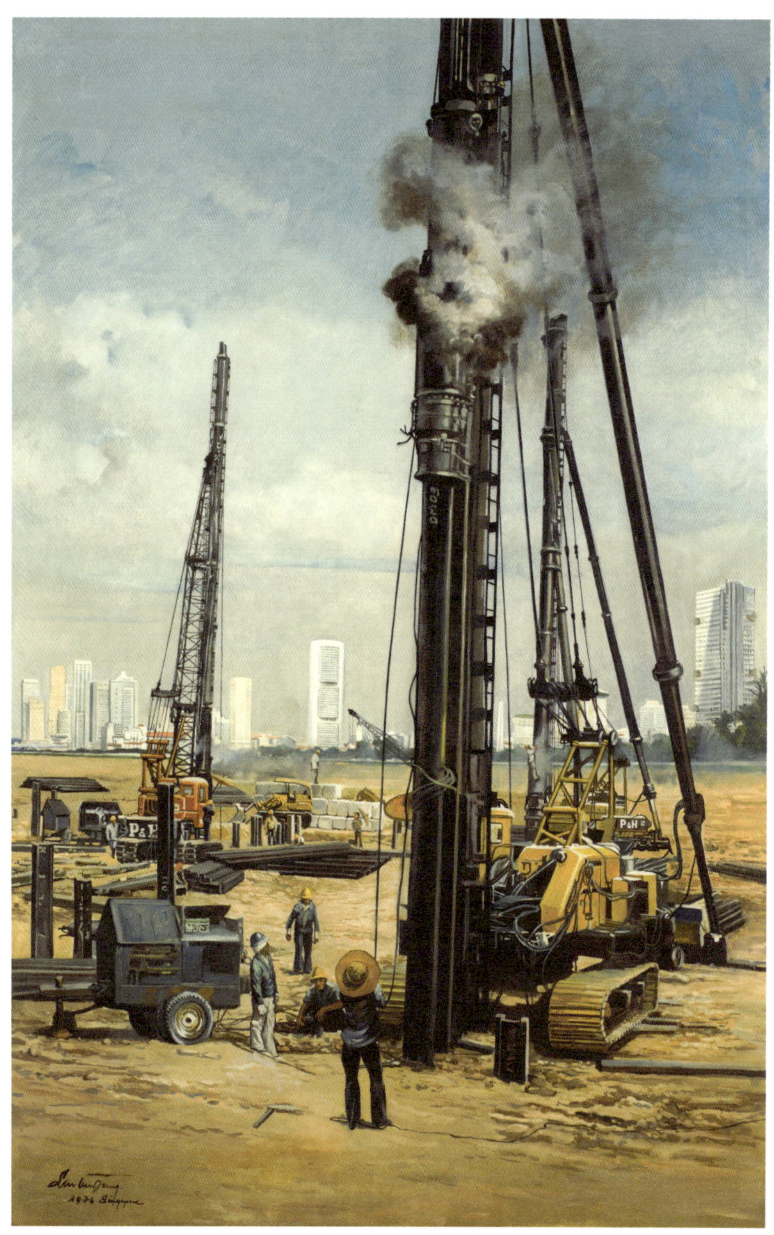

Lai Kui Fang
Construction of Sheares Bridge
1976
Oil on canvas, 202 × 132 cm
Gift of the Istana

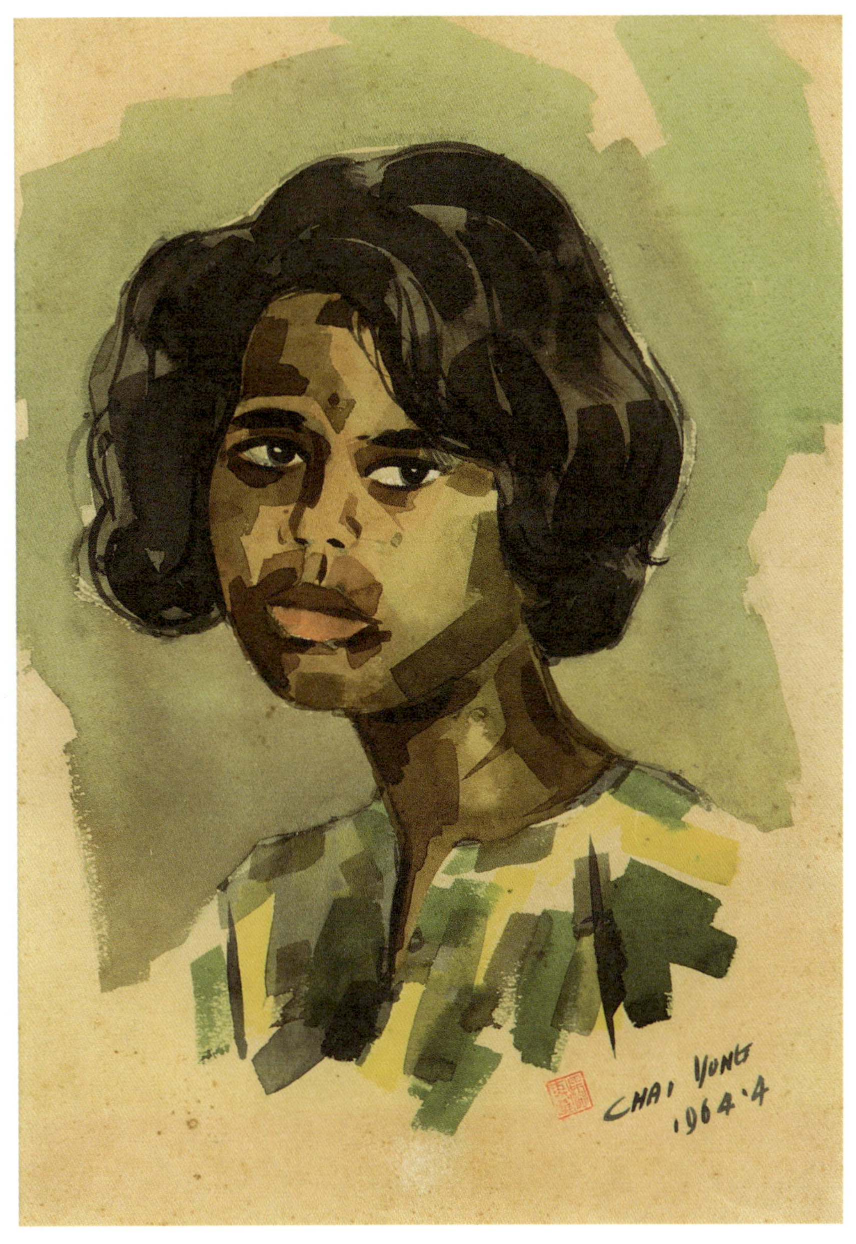

Hua Chai Yong
Portrait 1
1964
Watercolour on paper
38 × 27 cm

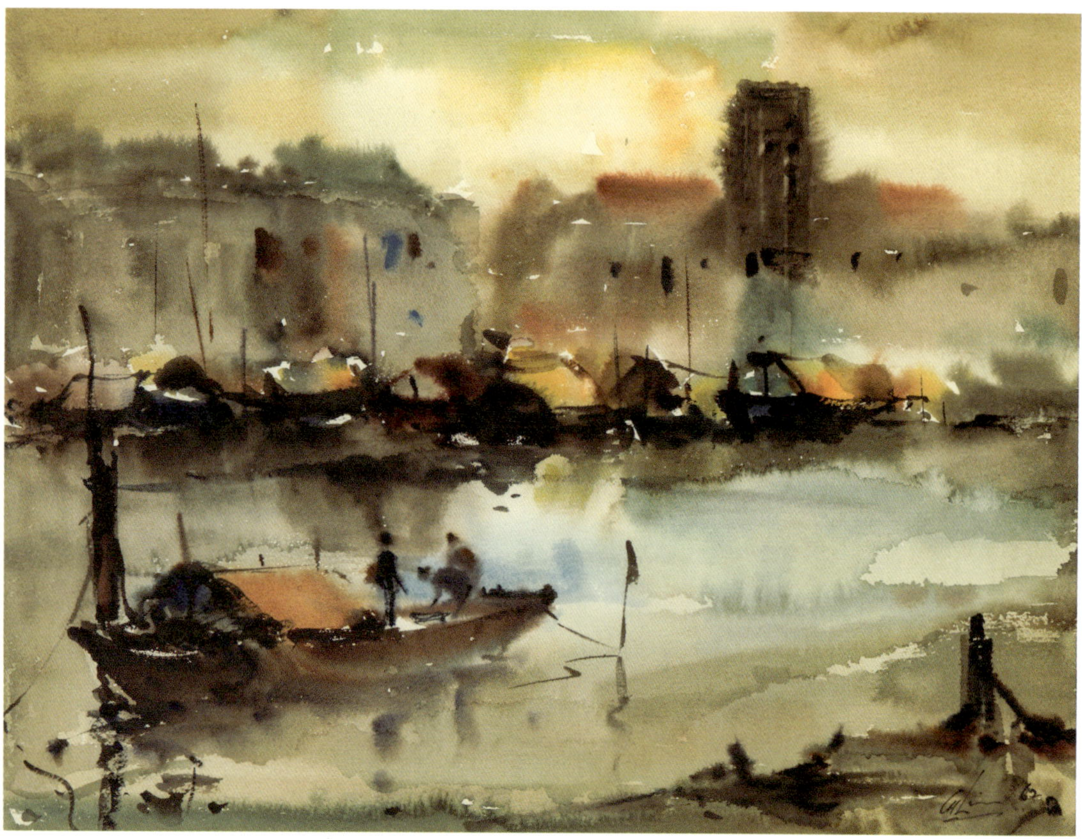

The Singapore River was a favourite scene of Lim Cheng Hoe and his contemporaries, a site they frequented during their regular group painting sessions. In this work, Lim has captured an ephemeral moment that suggests, rather than describes, the hustle and bustle of the river.

Lim Cheng Hoe. *Singapore River.* Late 1960s. Watercolour on paper, 33 × 43 cm.

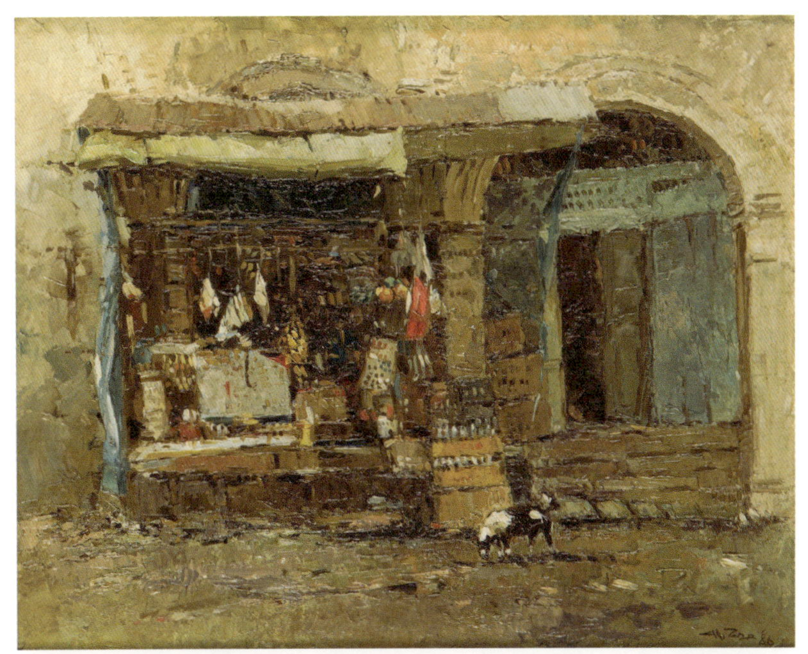

Ang Ah Tee
Mama Stall (Sophia Road)
1986
Oil on canvas
60 × 76 cm

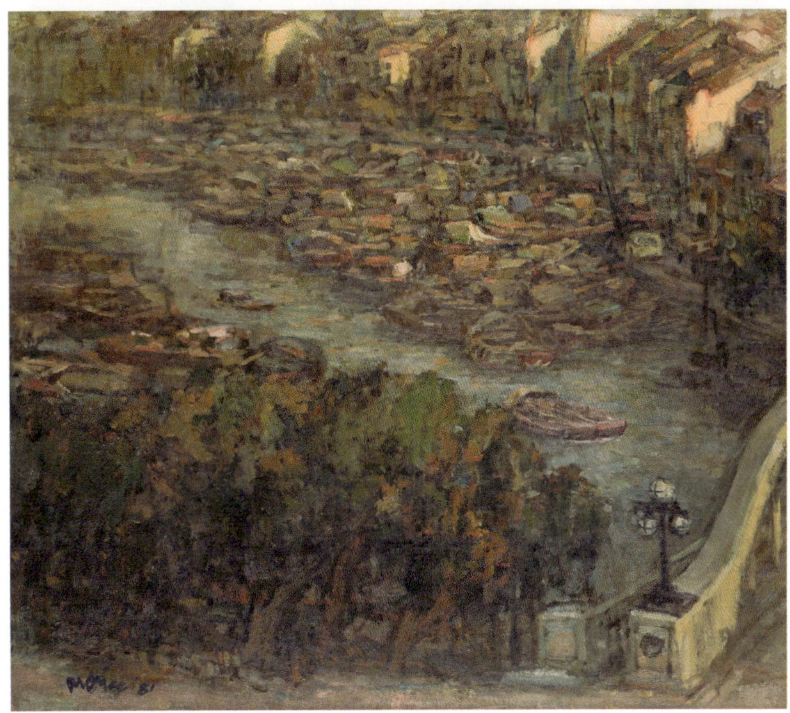

Tan Choh Tee
Singapore River
1981
Oil on canvas
73 × 82 cm

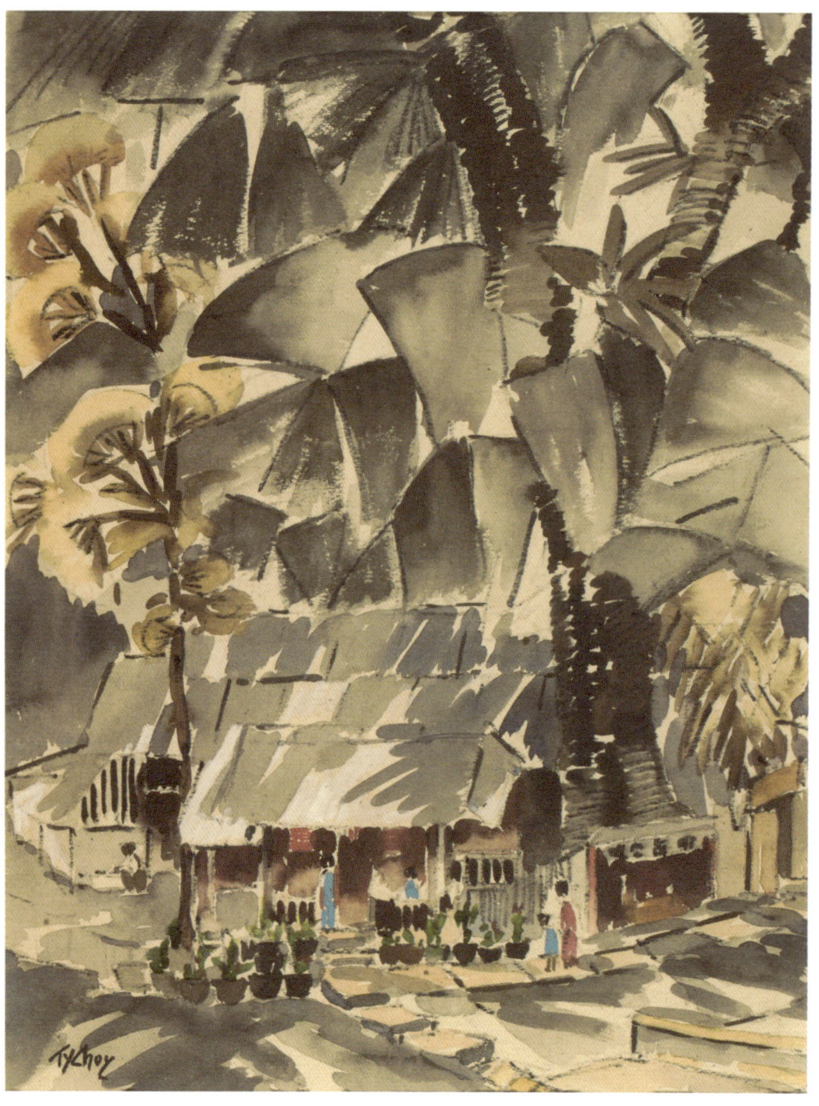

T.Y. Choy
Little Temple
Undated
Watercolour on paper
49 × 38 cm
Gift from the Loke Wan Tho Collection

OPPOSITE PAGE

Gog Sing Hooi
Thean Hock Keng Temple
1984
Watercolour on paper
72 × 54 cm

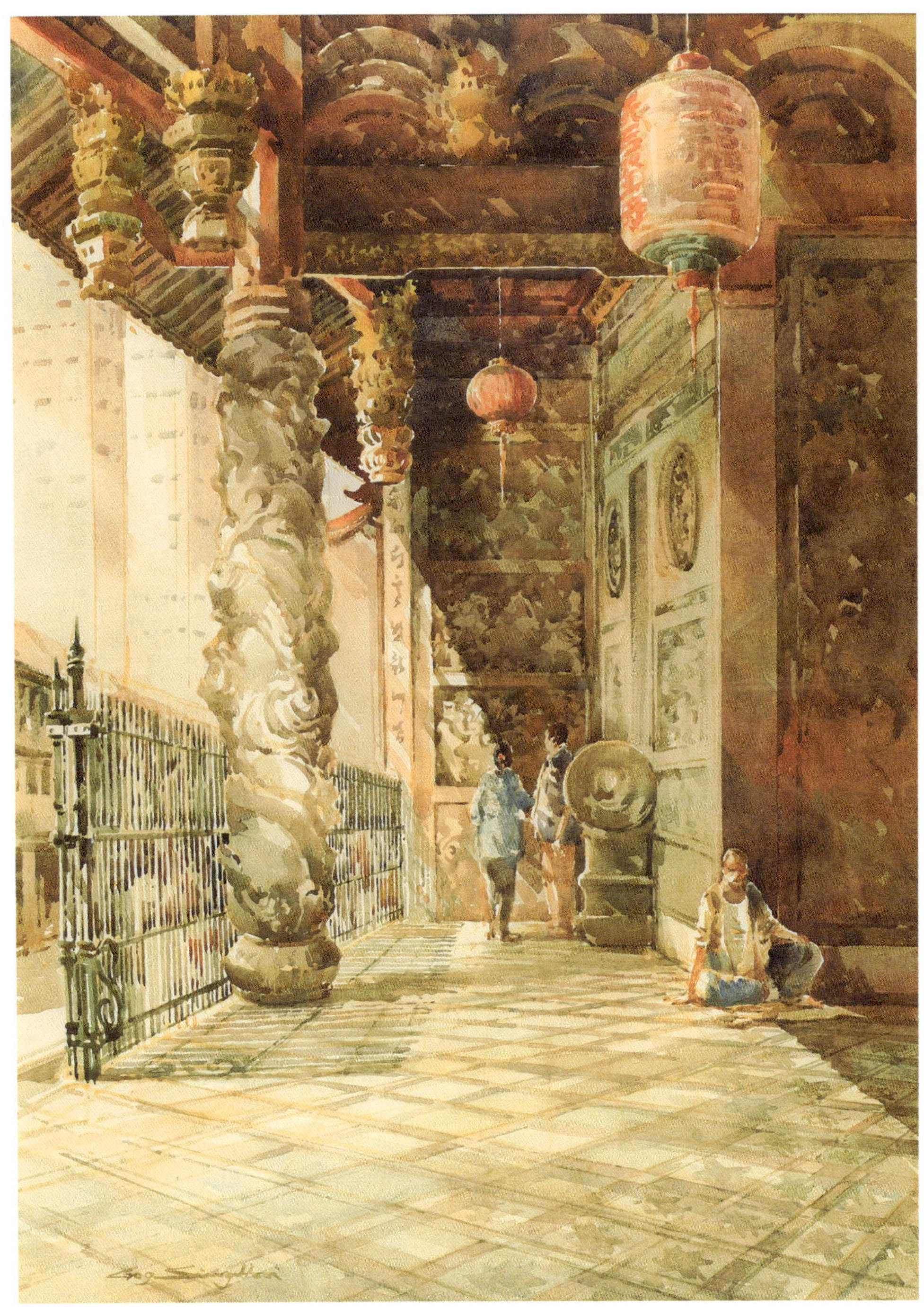

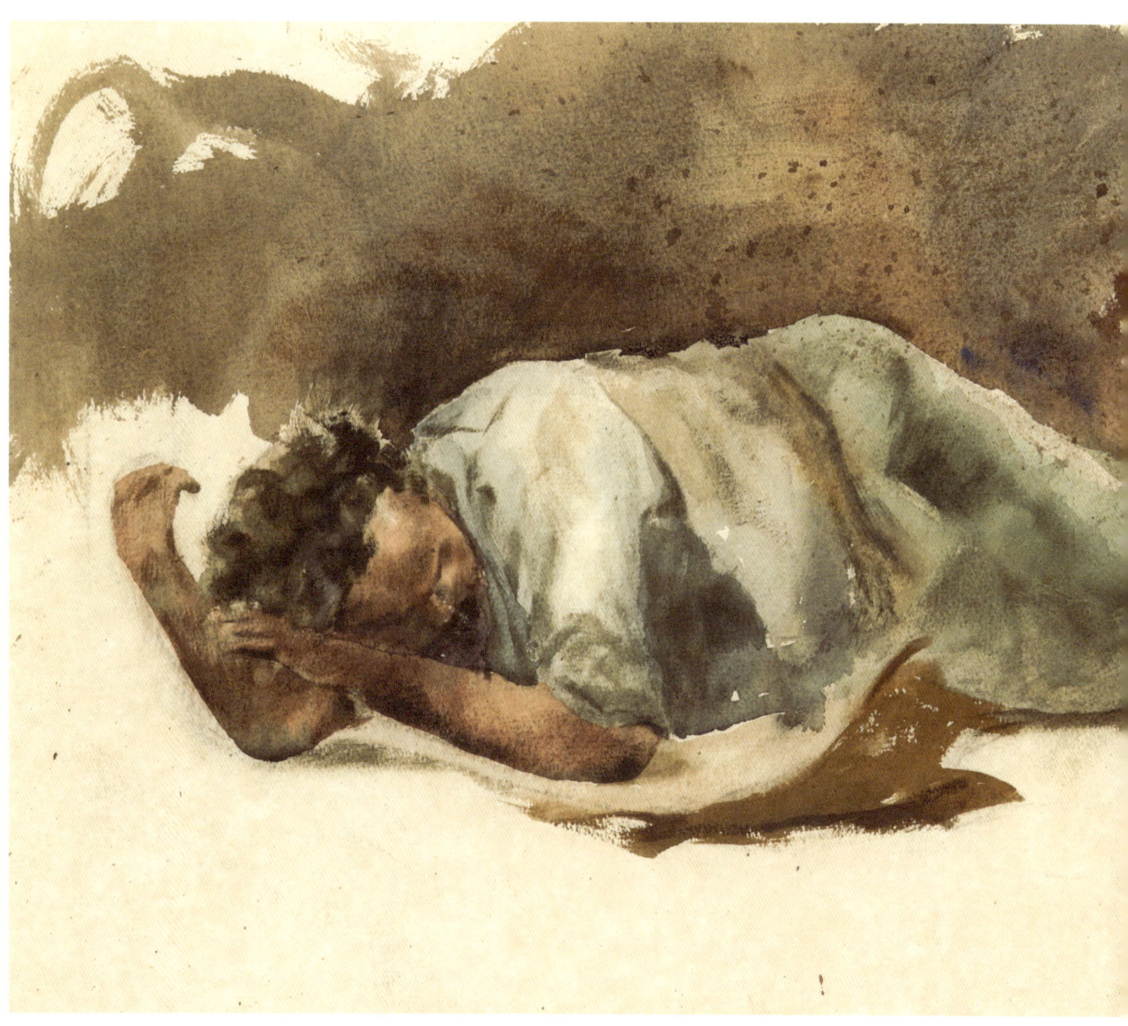

Drunkard is an early example of figurative watercolour painting by Ong Kim Seng. When he was young, Ong learnt art at the Equator Art Society, which believed in championing the cause of the ordinary man through realistic depictions of their plight. In this painting, the warm swathes of brown in the background seem to weigh heavily upon the drunkard, sinking him into a deep, inebriated stupor.

Ong Kim Seng. *Drunkard*. 1977. Watercolour on paper, 38 × 56 cm. Gift of the artist.

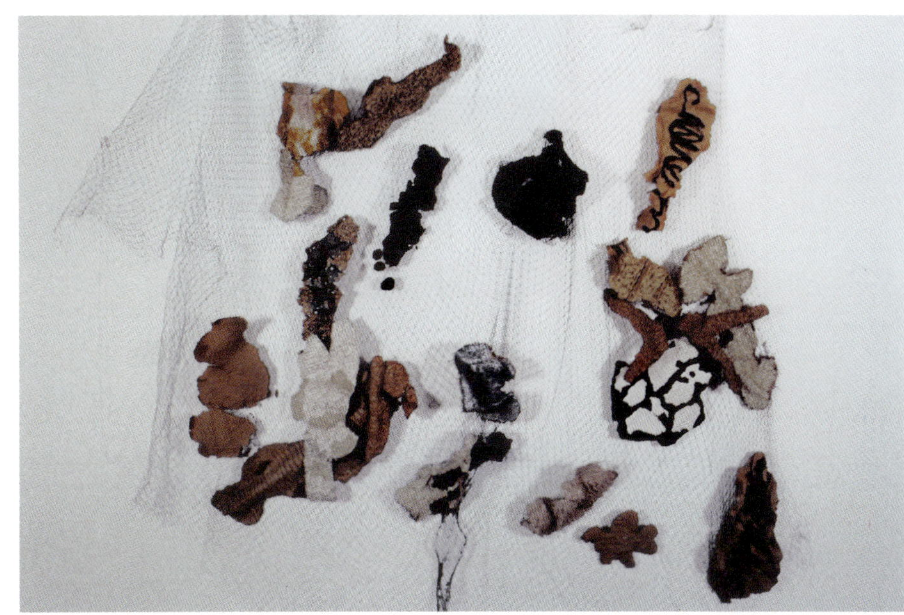

Picturesque representations of the Singapore River proliferated in the 1970s and 1980s, appearing on postcards, currency and souvenirs. Were Singapore artists uncritically producing works of this ilk? An exhibition titled *Not the Singapore River* sparked this debate in the newspapers and inspired this work. It is made of "paperdyesculp," a term the artist coined to refer to modelled dyed paper pulp. The title of the work further reveals Teo Eng Seng's tongue-in-cheek humour.

Teo Eng Seng. *The Net: Most Definitely the Singapore River*. 1986. Paperdyesculp and net, 350 × 350 cm. Gift of the artist.

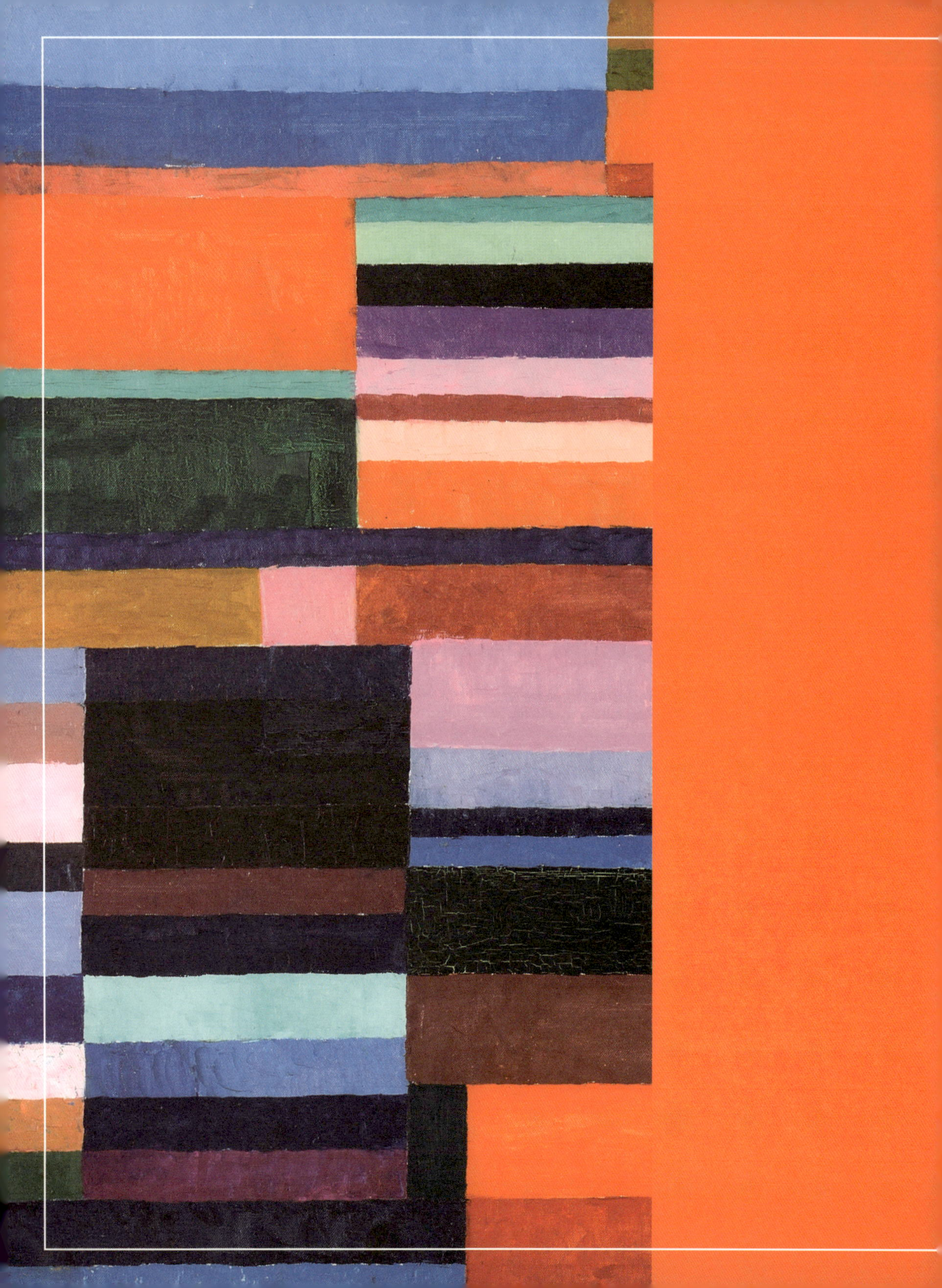

New Languages

In 1963, artist Ho Ho Ying declared, "Realism has passed its golden age; Impressionism has done its duty; Fauvism and Cubism are declining. Something new must turn up to succeed the unfinished task left by our predecessors." The new artistic language, the first Chairman of the Modern Art Society might have added, was abstraction.

Abstract art does not seek to reproduce physical reality. Instead it relies on pure form, colour and texture to convey meaning or emotion. Abstraction was espoused by a younger generation of artists who felt that realism could no longer reflect Singapore's rapid modernisation or aid in its artistic development. Some of these artists had trained overseas in the 1960s and 1970s. The groundwork for the rise of abstraction had, however, been laid down a decade before, as seen in the semi-abstract works of early migrant artists like Cheong Soo Pieng, Chen Wen Hsi, Lim Hak Tai and Yeh Chi Wei.

As modern art developed in the local and international scene from the 1970s, the physical form of an artwork, and the very materials used in its making, became the focus. Calling for a fresh perspective on the definition of painting and sculpture, some artists sought to reflect the modern industrialised age, while others grounded their art in local situations and explored how traditional art forms like ink and batik could be modernised.

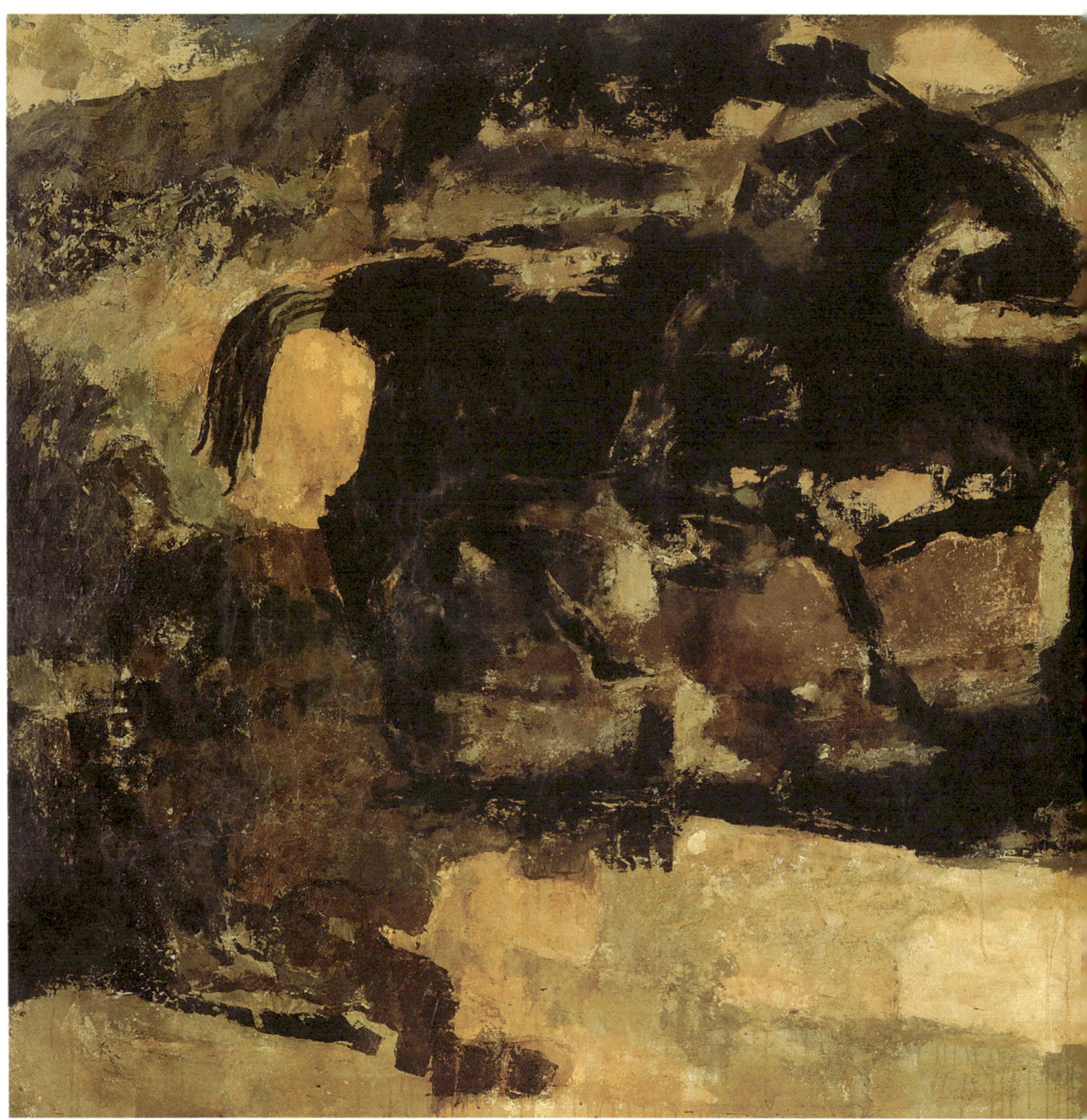

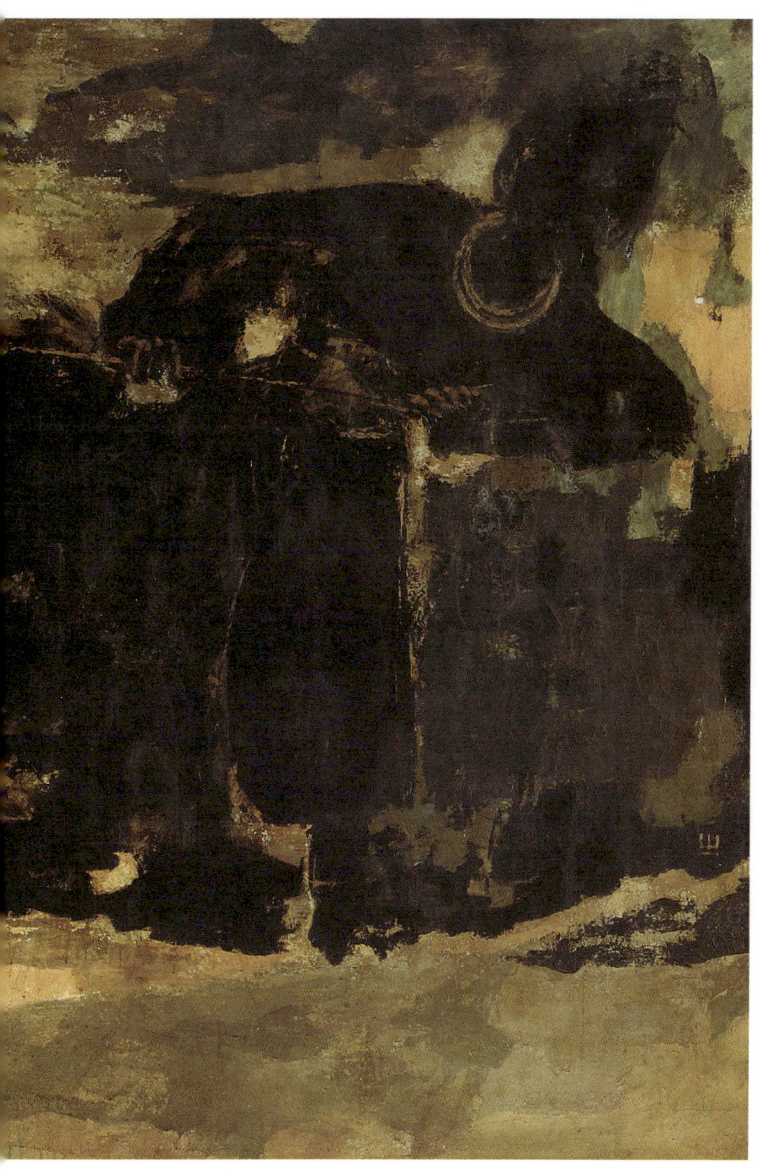

Yeh Chi Wei's style is informed by Western abstraction, Chinese archaism and Southeast Asian cultures. This work shows Yeh's move away from realistic representation. Its rich variety of textures evokes the time-worn appearance of ancient murals, while the dominant use of black echoes Chinese ink rubbings. The motif of the horse in the style of Han pictorial carvings can also be found in an earlier painting by Yeh, *Miao Girl Pulling A Horse.*

Yeh Chi Wei
Untitled (Pulling the Horse)
c. 1960s
Oil on canvas
122.5 × 219.7 cm
Gift of the family of Yeh Chi Wei

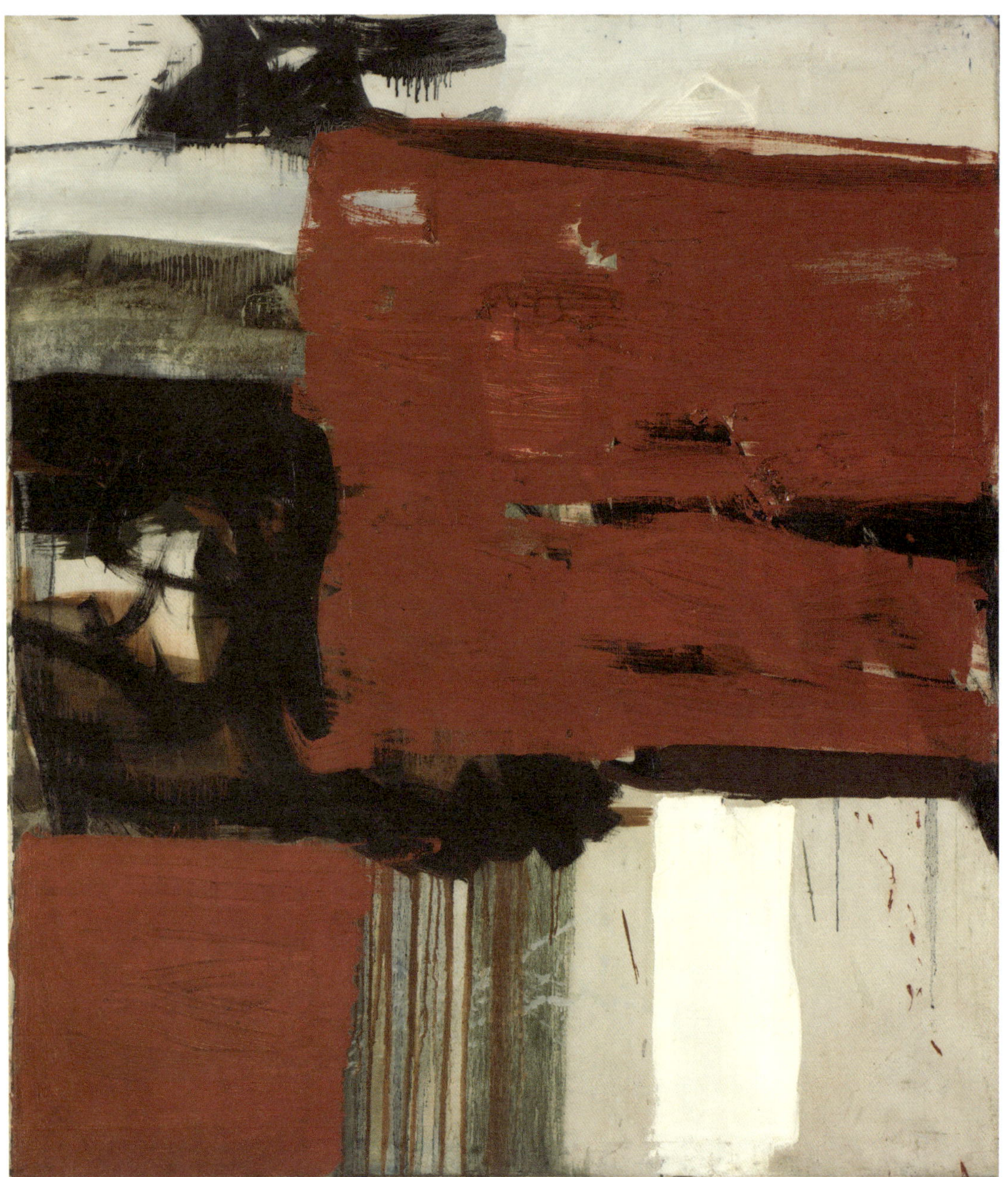

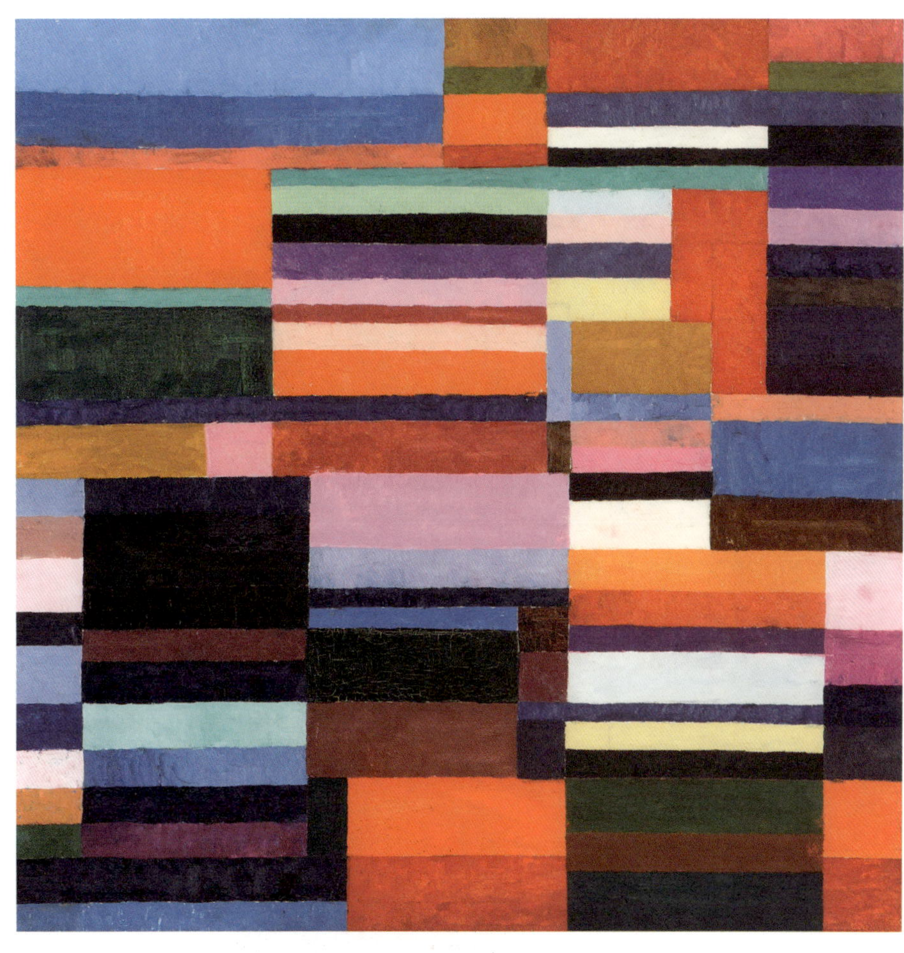

Choy Weng Yang
Horizontals I
1977
Oil on canvas
92 × 92 cm
Gift of the artist

OPPOSITE PAGE

Goh Beng Kwan
Black Afternoon
1963
Mixed media on canvas
126 × 111 cm

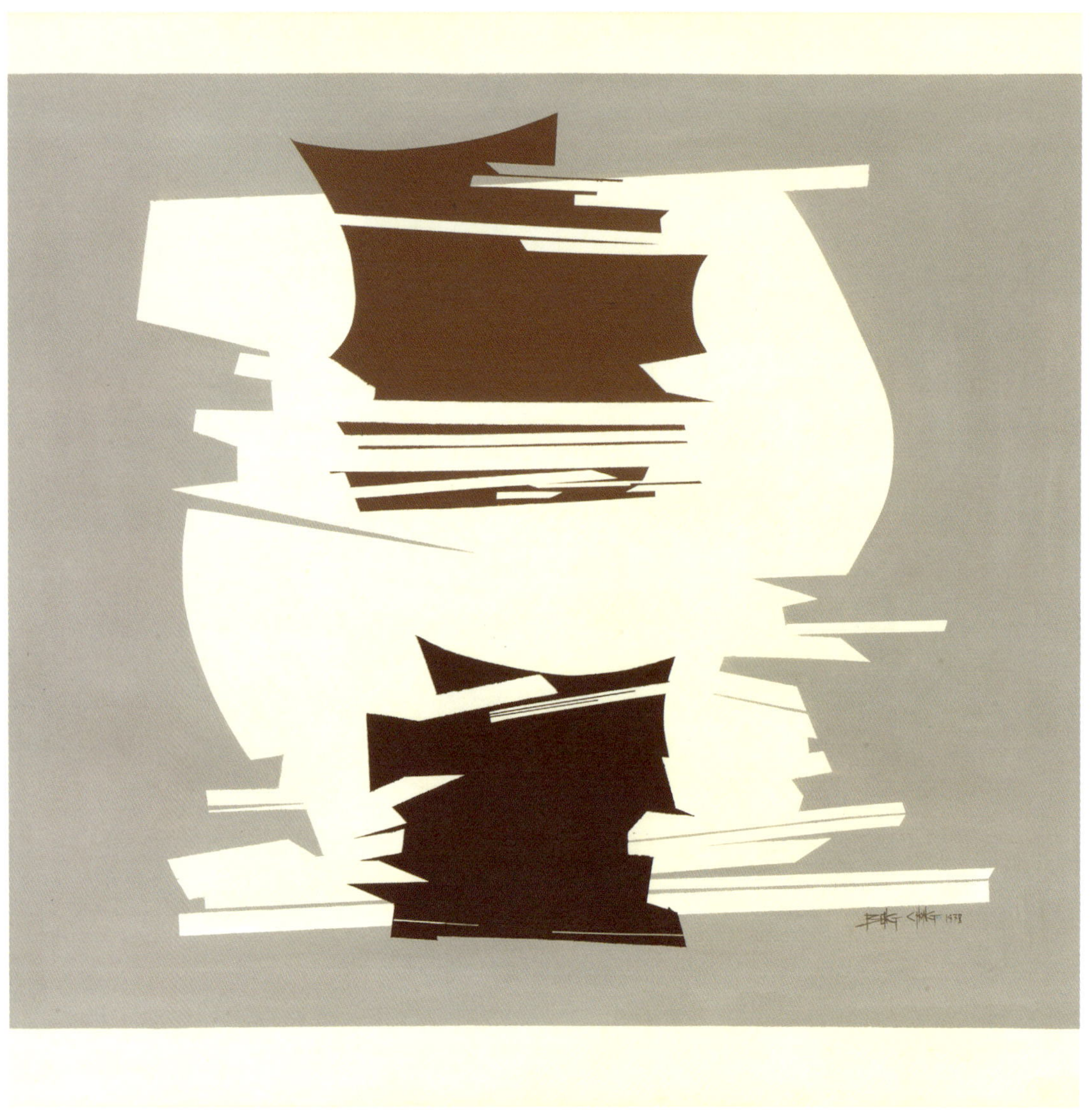

Wee Beng Chong
Conflict
1978
Enamel paint on masonite board
121 × 121 cm
Gift of the artist

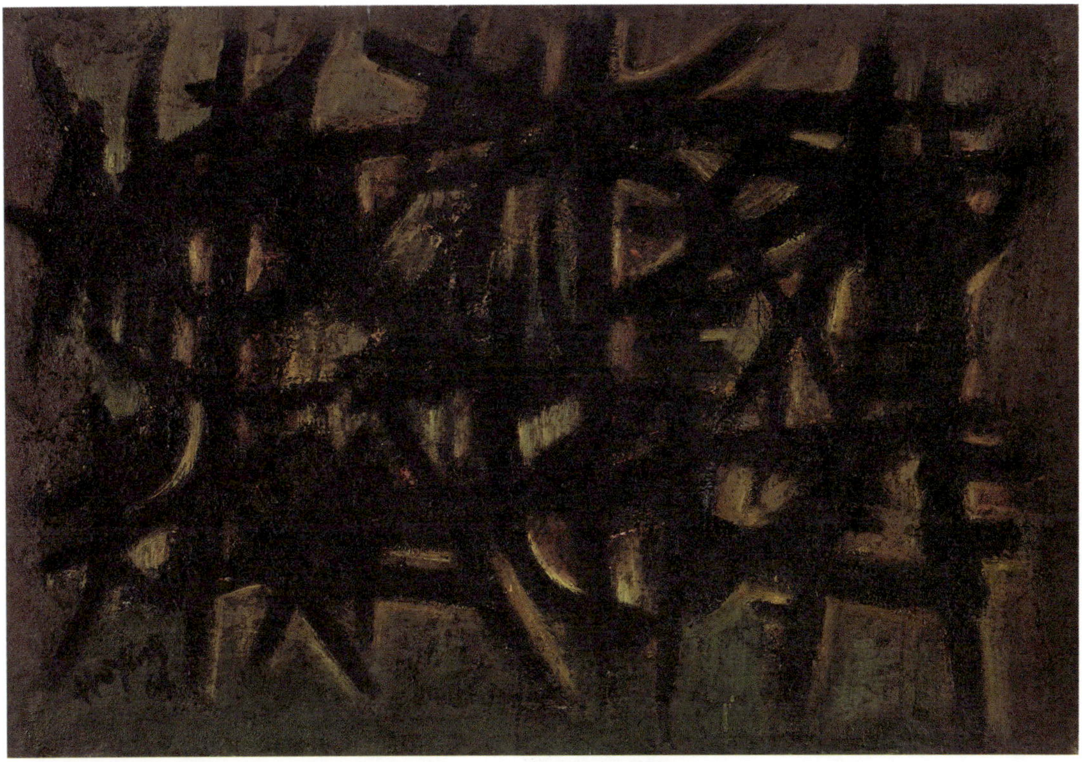

The dynamism and tension conveyed by this mass of interlocking forms stands in contrast to the glow beneath them, which seems to hint at an unknown, mysterious or even metaphysical realm. During the late 1950s and 1960, Ho Ho Ying championed abstract art as the most relevant art form for modern Singapore.

Ho Ho Ying. *Untitled*. 1964. Oil on canvas laid on board, 74 × 109.5 cm.

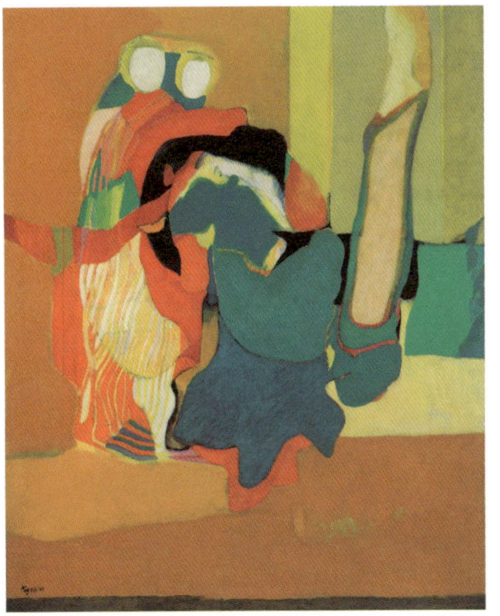

Thomas Yeo
Yellow Rider
1967
Acrylic on canvas
126 × 100 cm
Collection of the artist

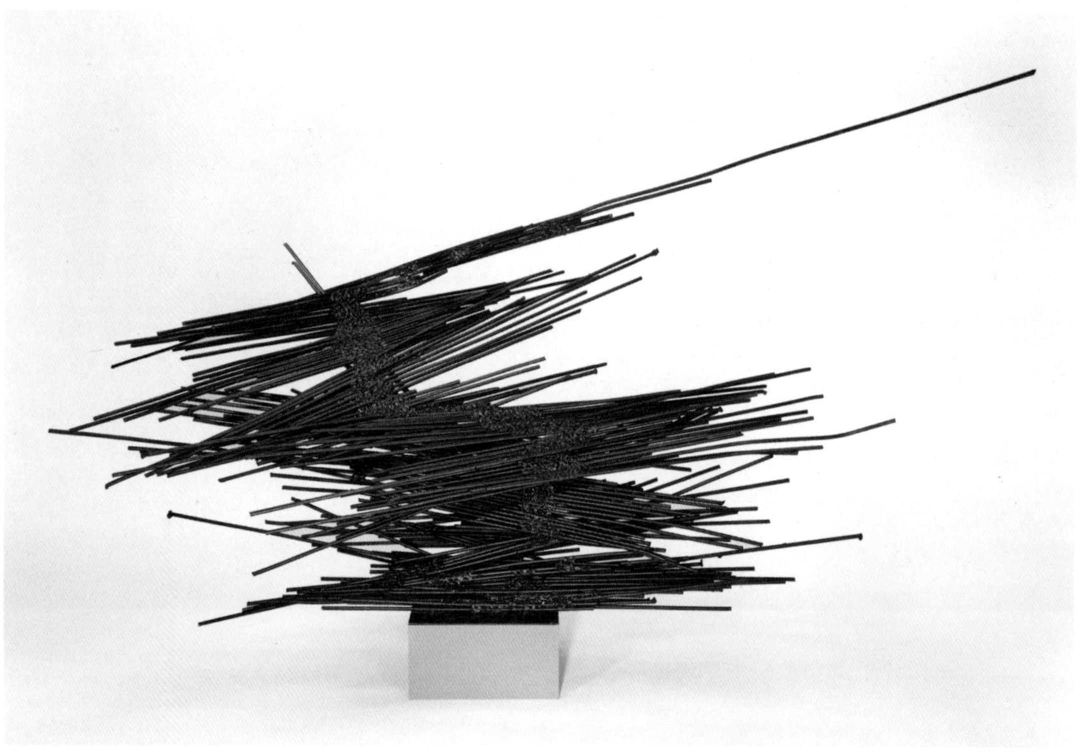

Tan Teng Kee
Space Sculpture No. 1
1976
Metal
107 × 228 × 123 cm
Gift of the artist

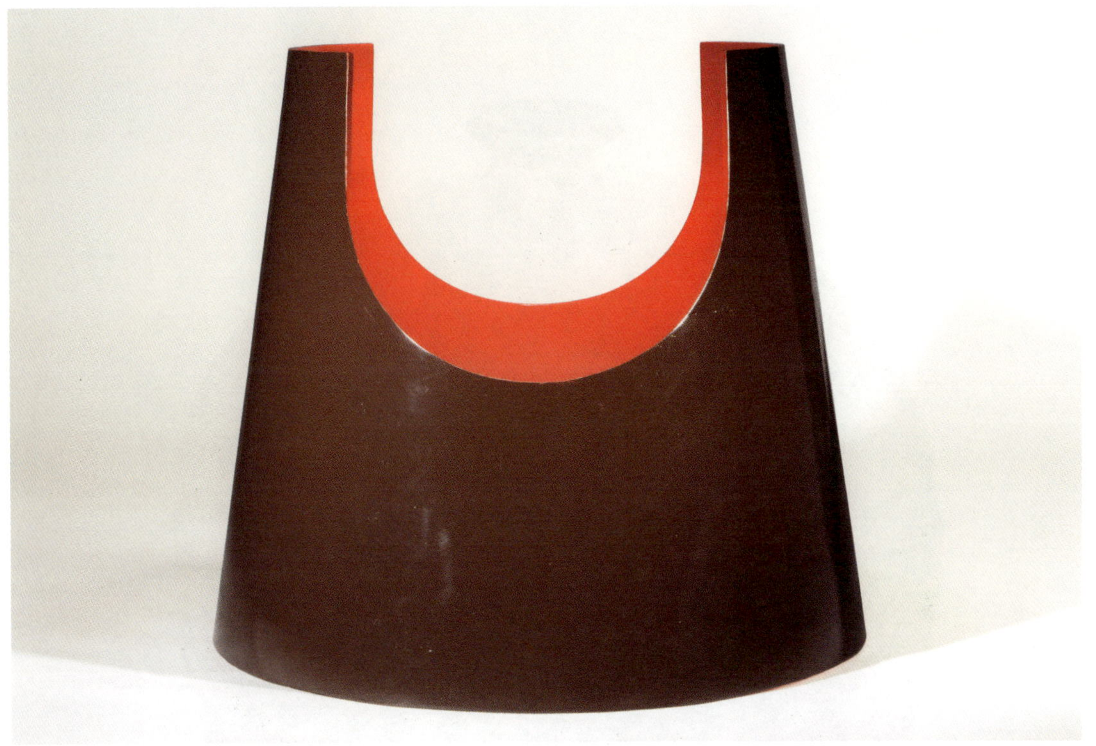

In this sculpture, Kim Lim employs roundness to contain and negate space. Lim was always concerned about how people would relate to her works, and rigorously explored how space, rhythm and light could be expressed with materials. Apart from an interest in European artists like the modernist sculptor Constantin Brancusi, she also professed "a great empathy for Eastern art of the past—for instance, to [sic] the non-verbal experience of the Zen Garden."

Kim Lim. *Echoes*. 1967. Stainless steel, enamel paint and zinc coating, 77 × 80 × 80 cm. Gift of William Turnbull.

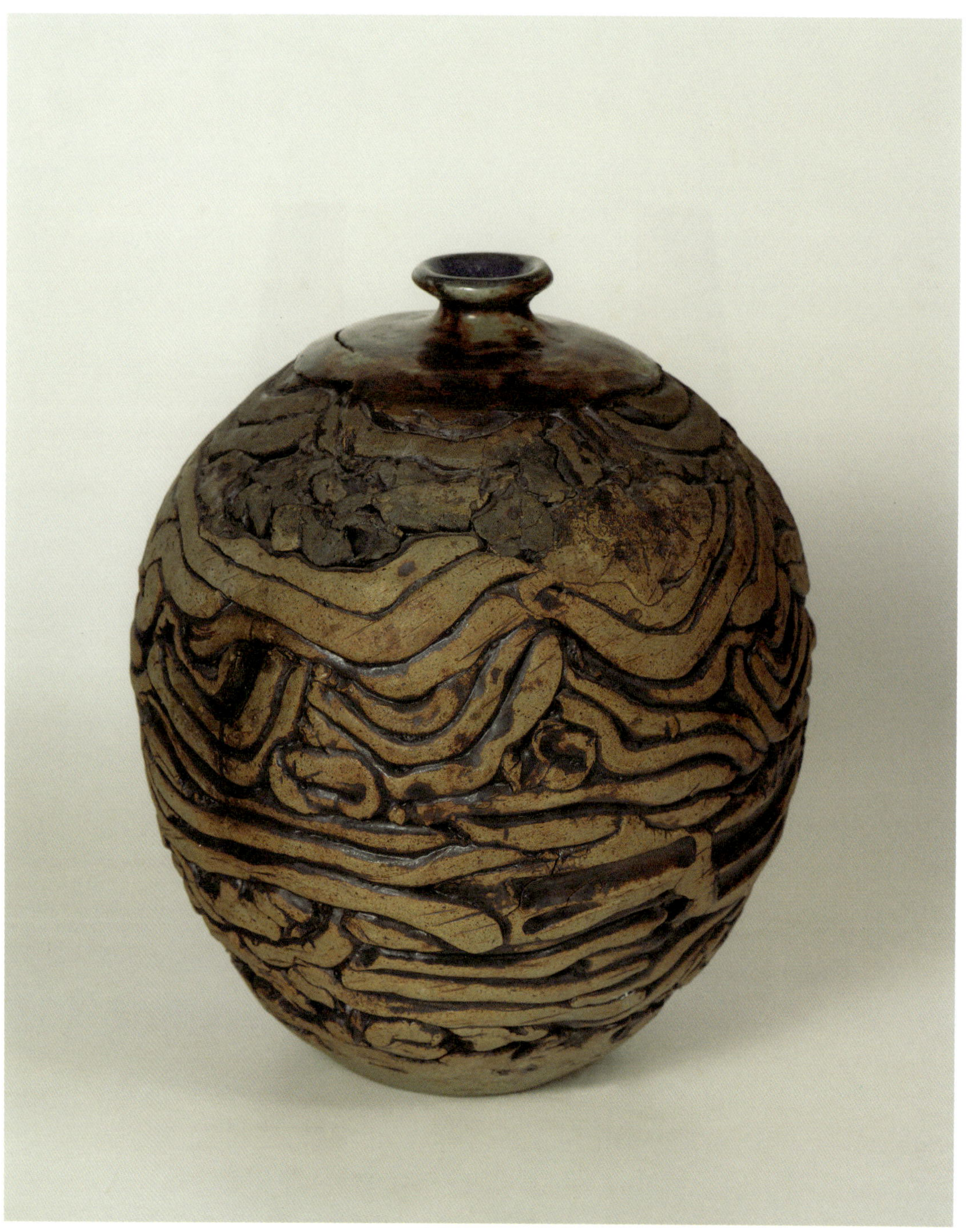

How is the interior world of an artist expressed? In this painting, the artist's mind is seen as a creative force comprising an interplay between the psychological, scientific and spiritual. A dream-like meditative atmosphere is created through soothing shades of blue, soft and wavy lines that recall pulses in an electrocardiogram, and a surrealistic rendition of a human face.

Abdul Ghani Hamid. *The Face in Meditation.* 1975. Oil on canvas, 86 × 61 cm. Gift of the artist.

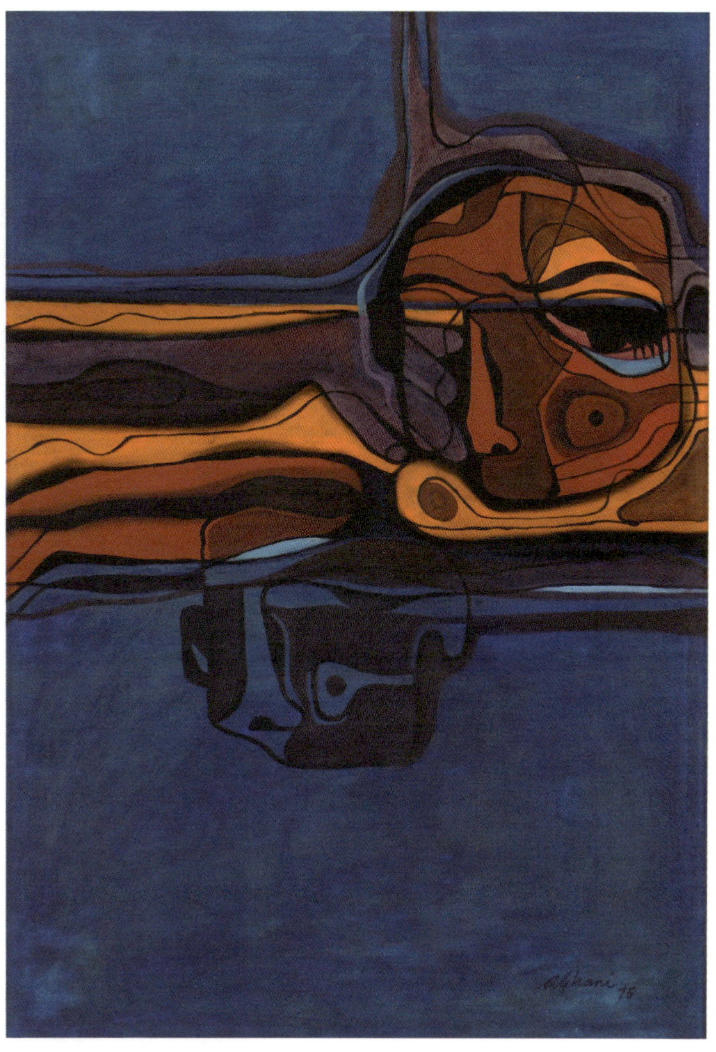

OPPOSITE PAGE

Iskandar Jalil seldom creates with a definite endpoint in mind. Instead, he often speaks of the importance of understanding one's materials, allowing them to guide one in the process of sculpting. First Coiled Pottery embodies Iskandar's interest in surface textures, the manipulation of which has transformed a functional vessel into a modern aesthetic object.

Iskandar Jalil. *First Coiled Pottery.* 1960. Clay, 35 × 35 × 35 cm. Collection of the artist.

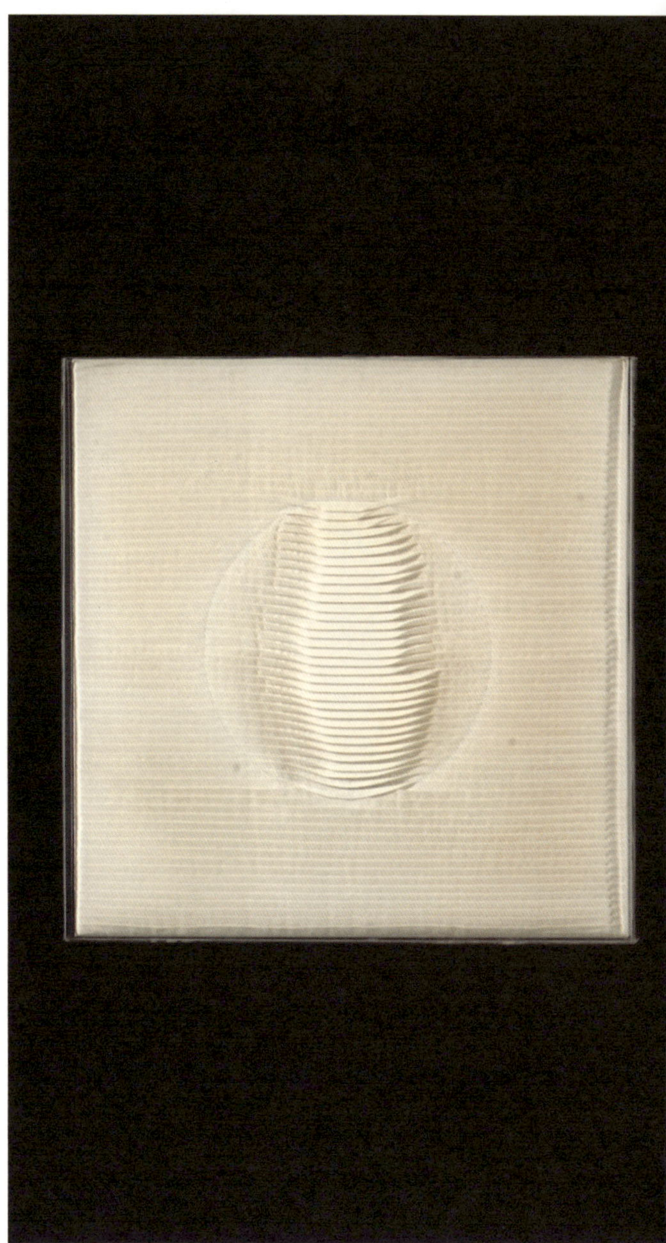

Eng Tow
Bowls
1979
Cloth and thread
62.5 × 61.5 cm each

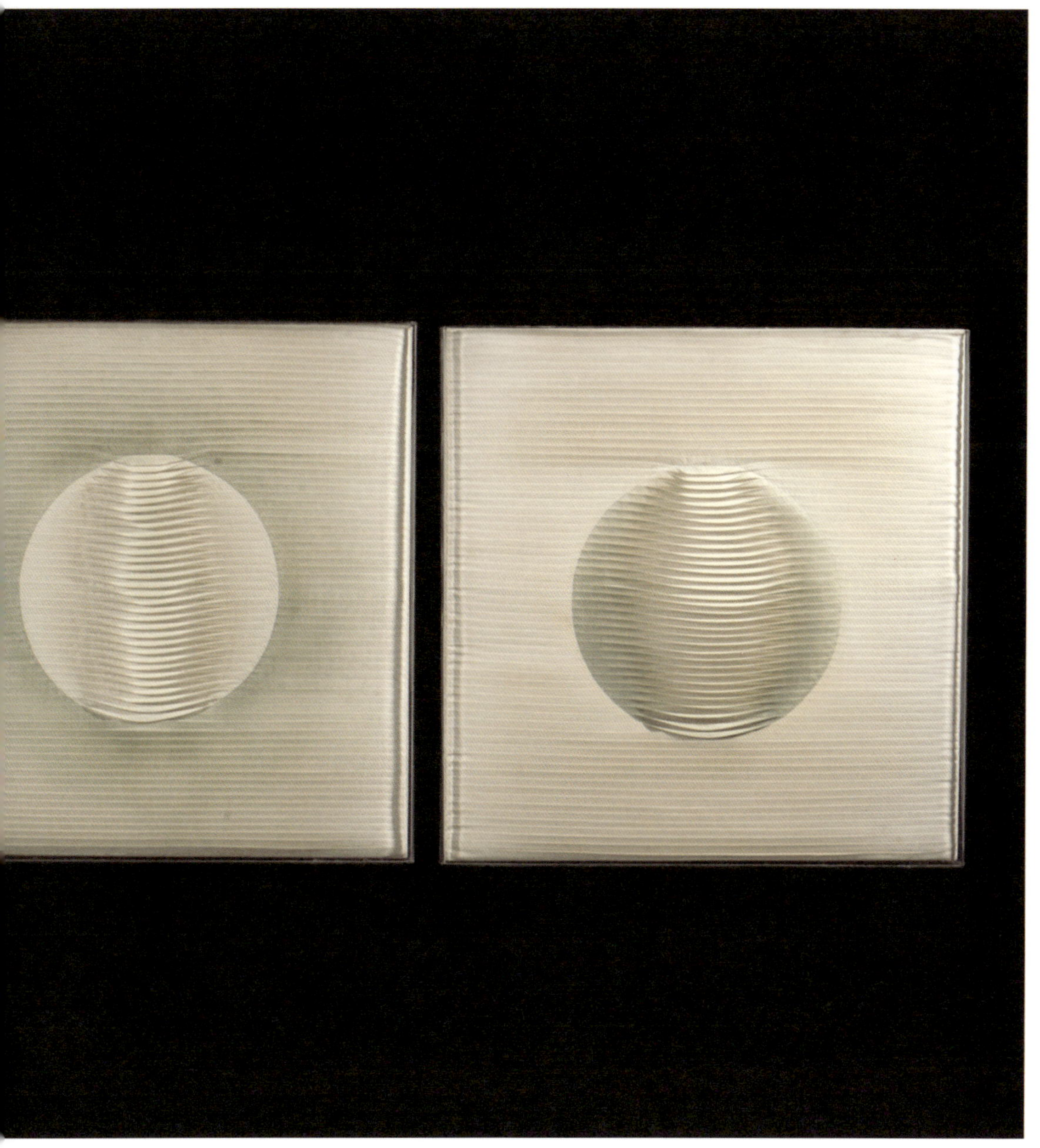

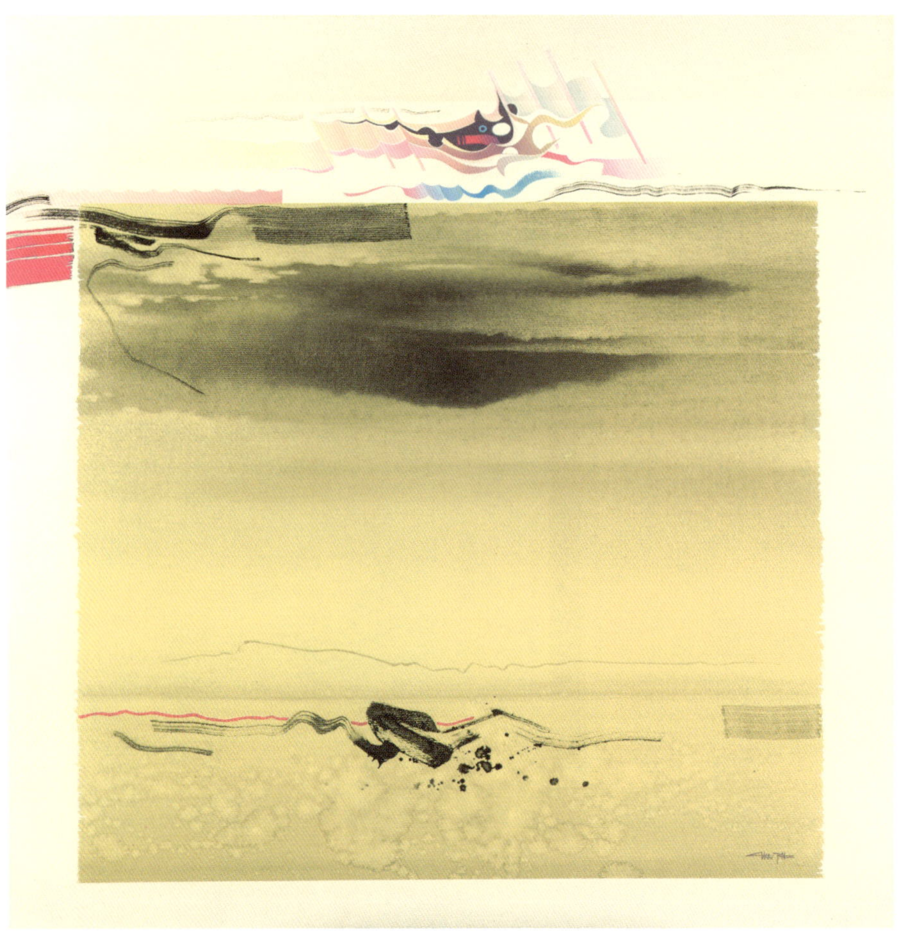

Tay Chee Toh
Golden Shadow
1985
Acrylic on canvas
122 × 122 cm

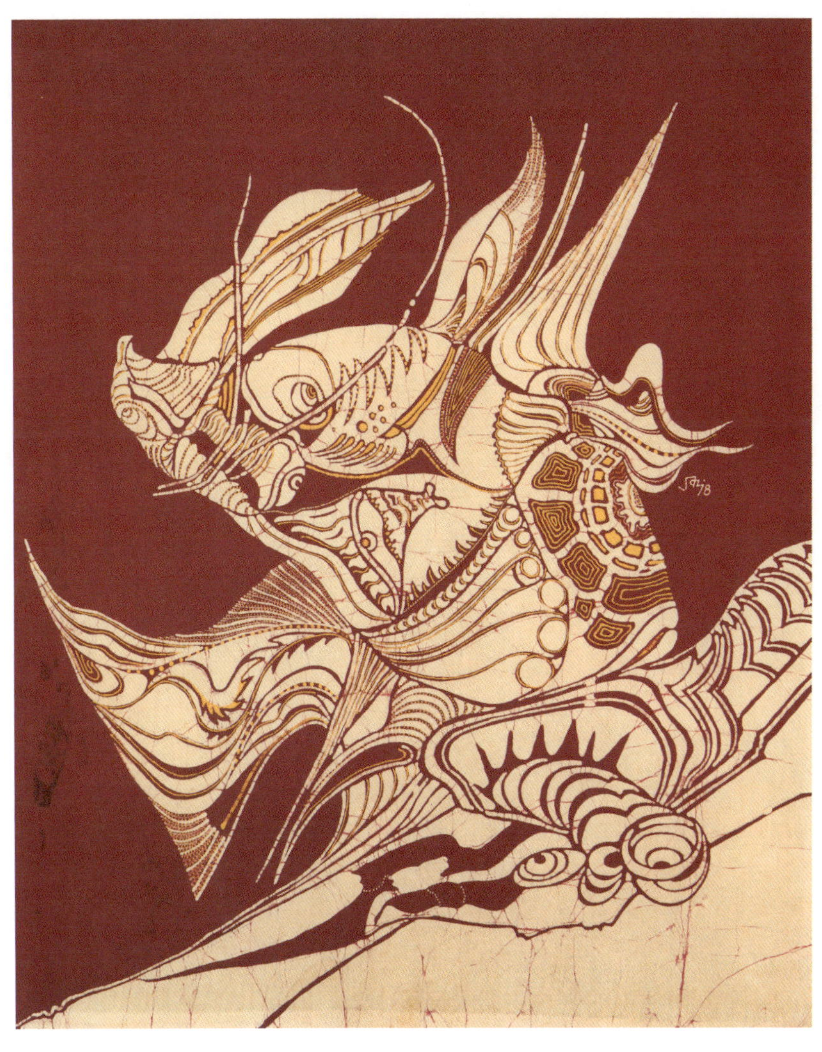

Sarkasi Said Tzee
Fish
1978
Batik
101 × 83 cm

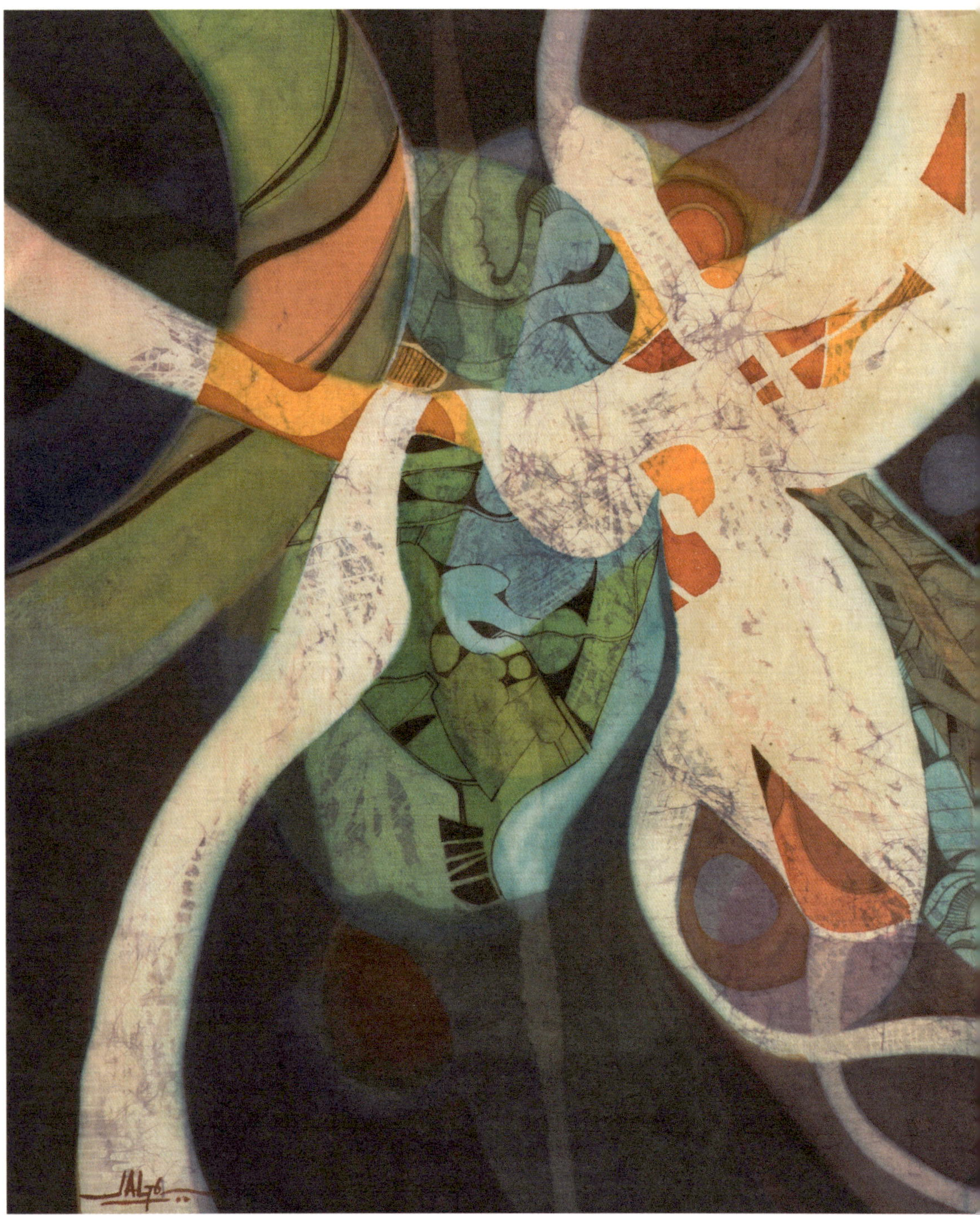

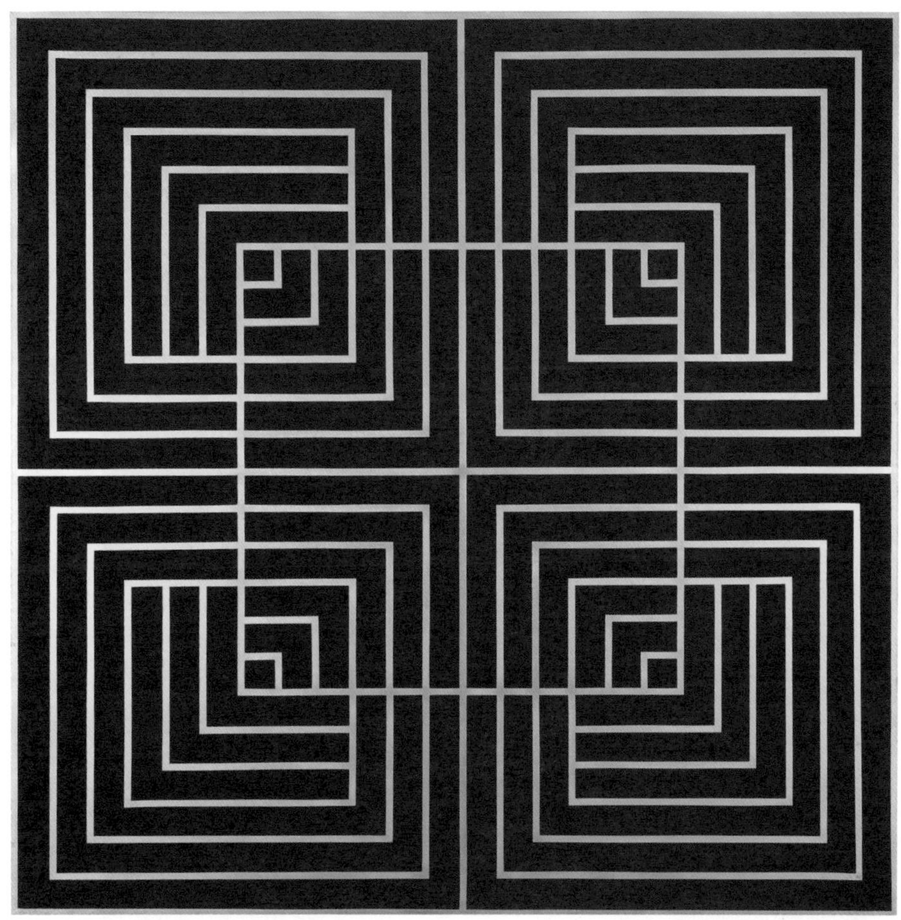

Anthony Poon
Black and White
1970s
Acrylic on canvas
186 × 186 cm

Jaafar Latiff
Wandering Series
1976
Batik
100 × 100 cm
Gift of the artist

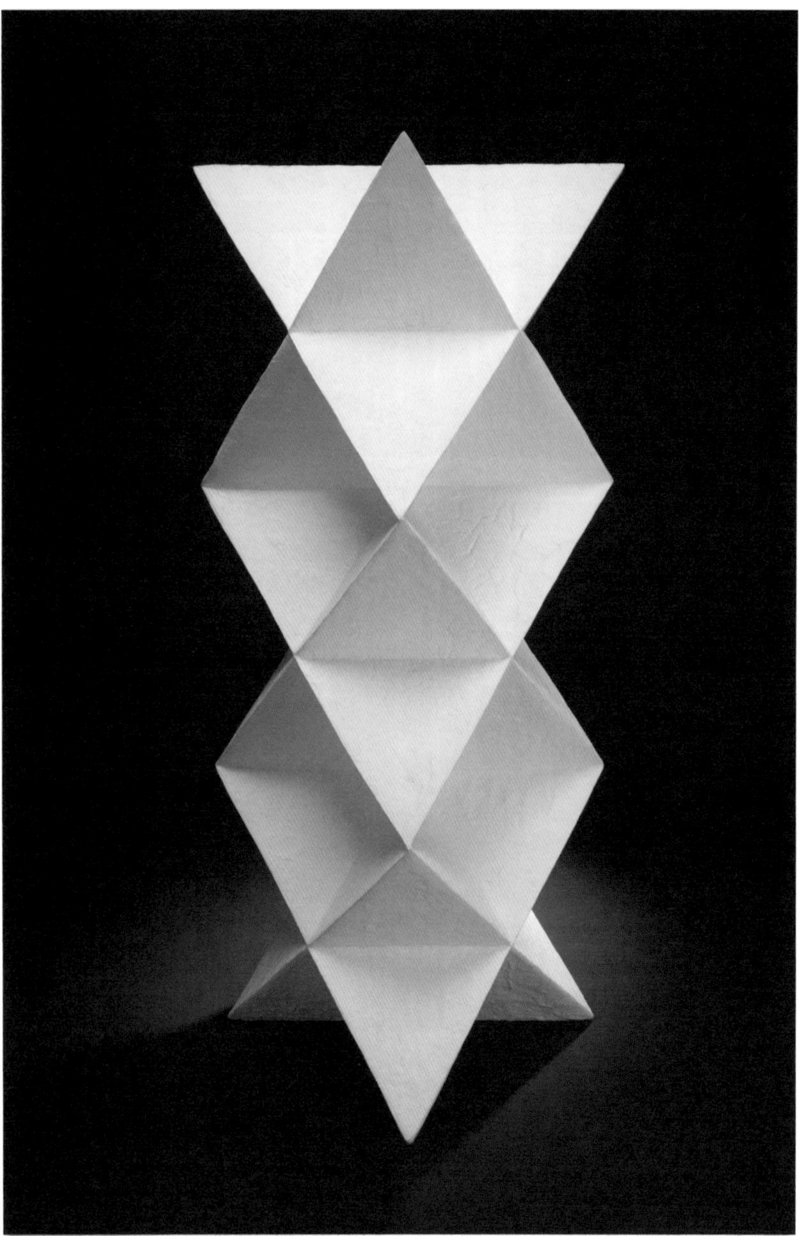

Han Sai Por
Tetrahedron-tetrahedron Interpenetration
1989
Fibreglass
184 × 62 × 62 cm

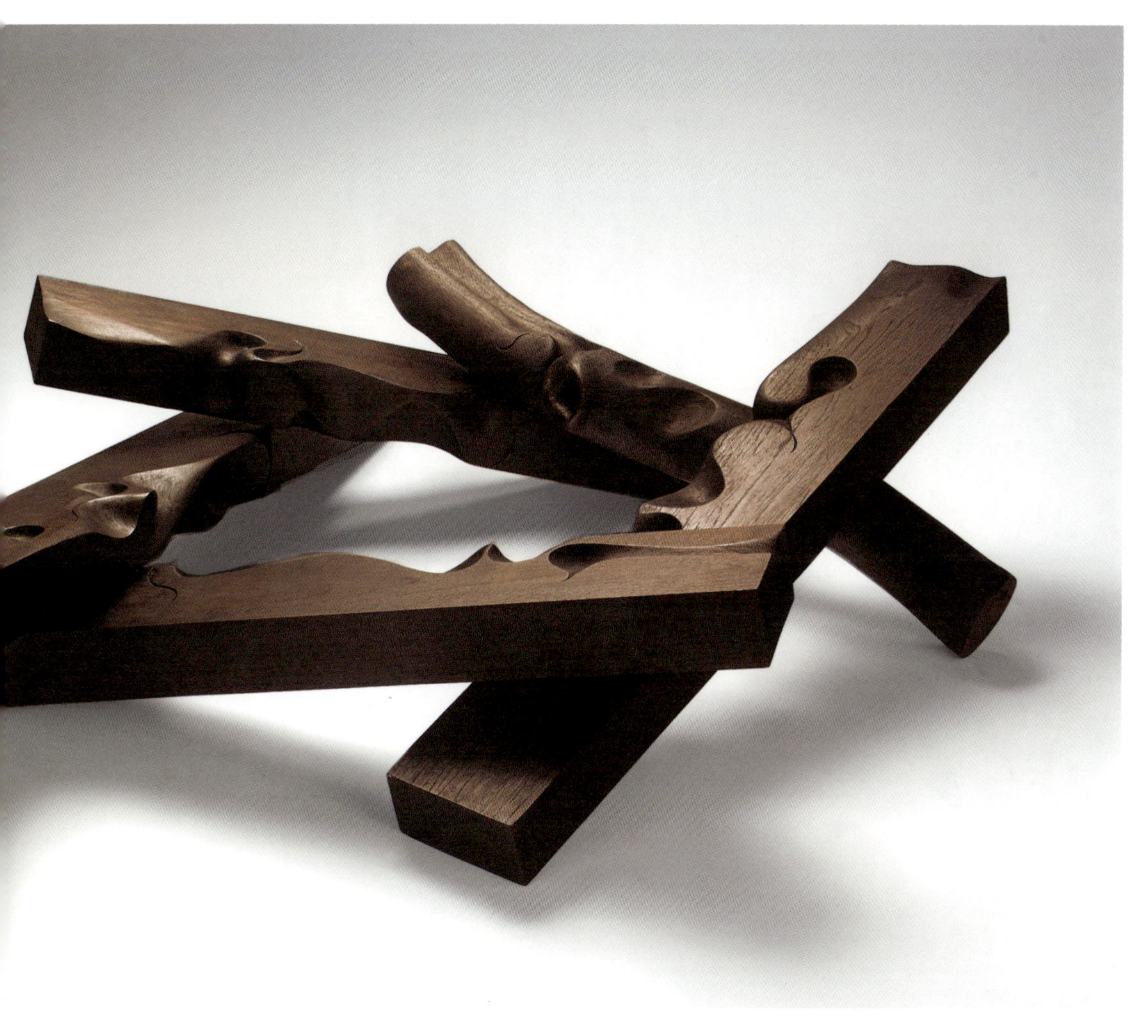

Chong Fah Cheong
Family (reworked into *Family and One*)
1985
Teak
35 × 137.5 × 122 cm

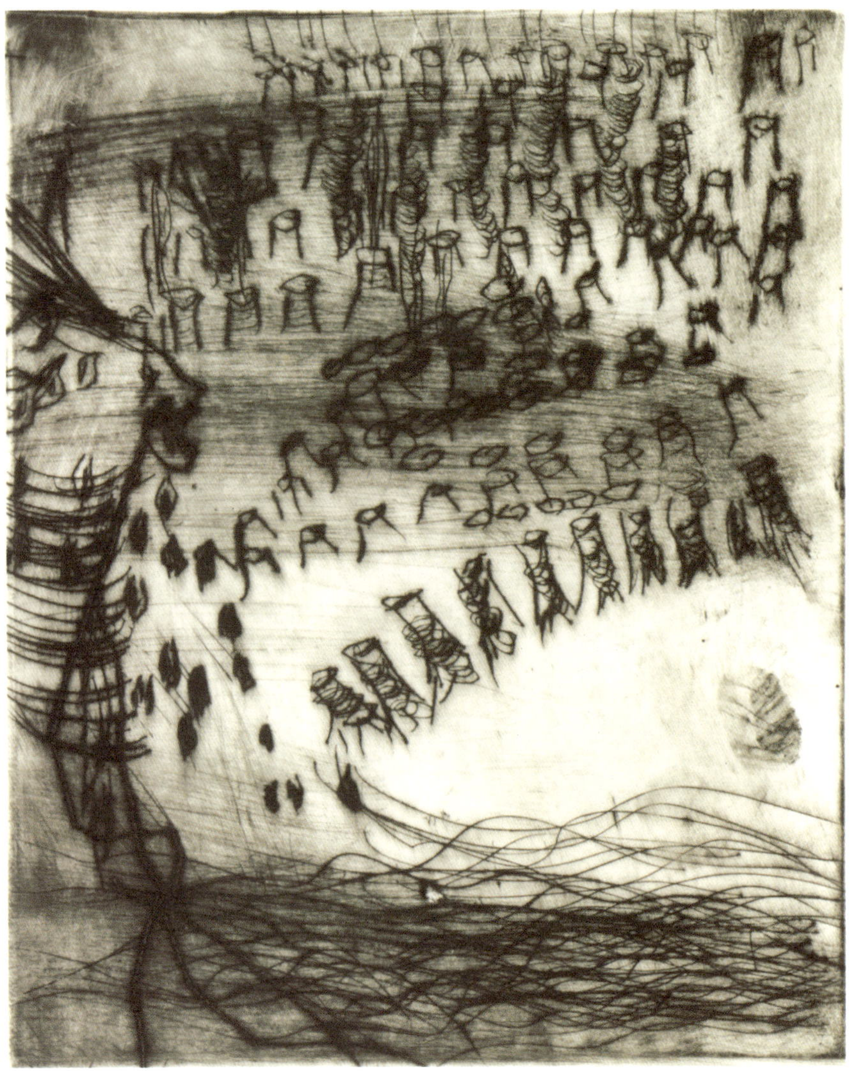

Chng Seok Tin
Following Trends
1993
Monoprint on paper
25 × 19 cm
Collection of Singapore Art Museum

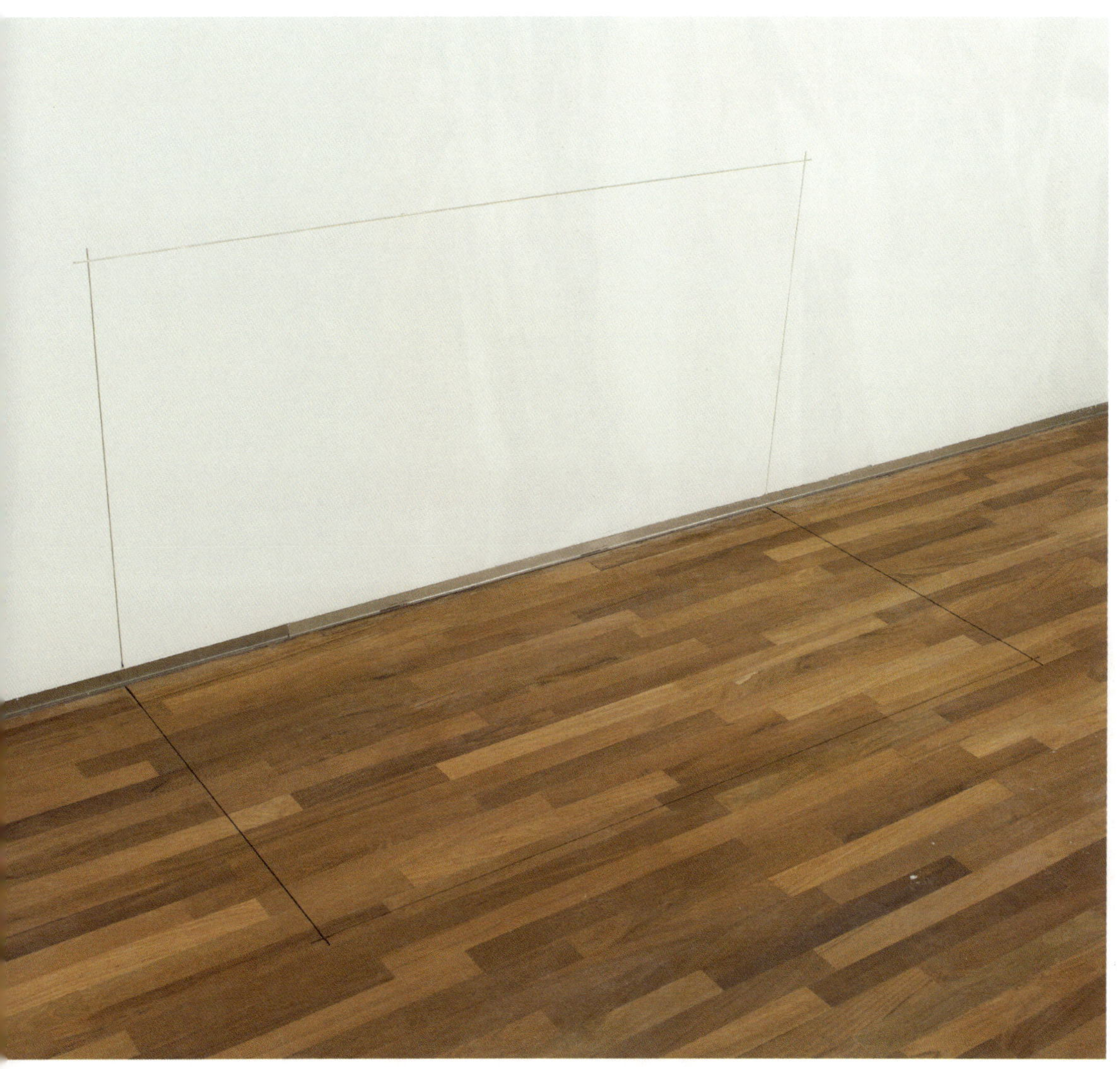

In 1972, Cheo Chai Hiang submitted a proposal for the Modern Art Society's annual exhibition, comprising instructions for a blank square measuring 5' x 5' to be drawn over the space of a wall and adjoining floor. This became an early example of conceptual art in Singapore. The work was ultimately not shown; Cheo recreated it in 2015 as 5' x 5' (Inched Deep) for the National Gallery Singapore, making an incision into the history of Singapore art.

Cheo Chai Hiang. *5' x 5' (Inched Deep).* 1972, remade for display in 2015. Mixed media, 150 × 150 cm.

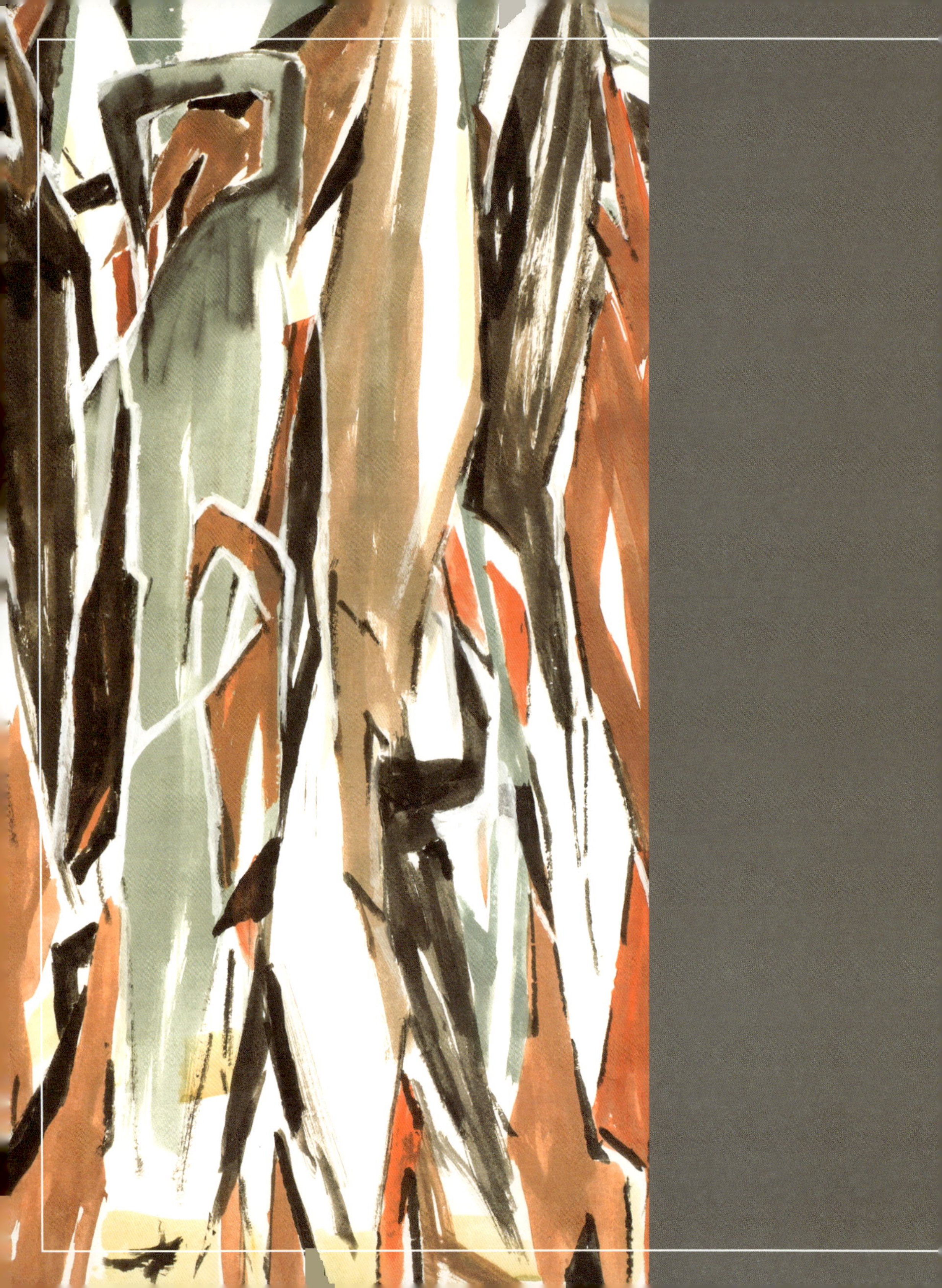

Tradition Unfettered

The development of Chinese ink in Singapore is as much a story of continuity as it is of transformation.

For most of the 20th century, migrant scholars and artists taught calligraphy and ink painting to a younger generation. While beholding the longstanding aesthetic legacies of Chinese ink, these artists were also concerned with how Southeast Asian scenes could be depicted, and whether the realist sensibility associated with modernisation could be infused into ink painting.

Innovations were led by some of these migrant artists, as seen in the example of Chen Wen Hsi, who integrated qualities of Chinese ink painting and Western modern art in his works. This local strand which we might call "Singapore ink" has been developed by a group of younger painters since the 1960s.

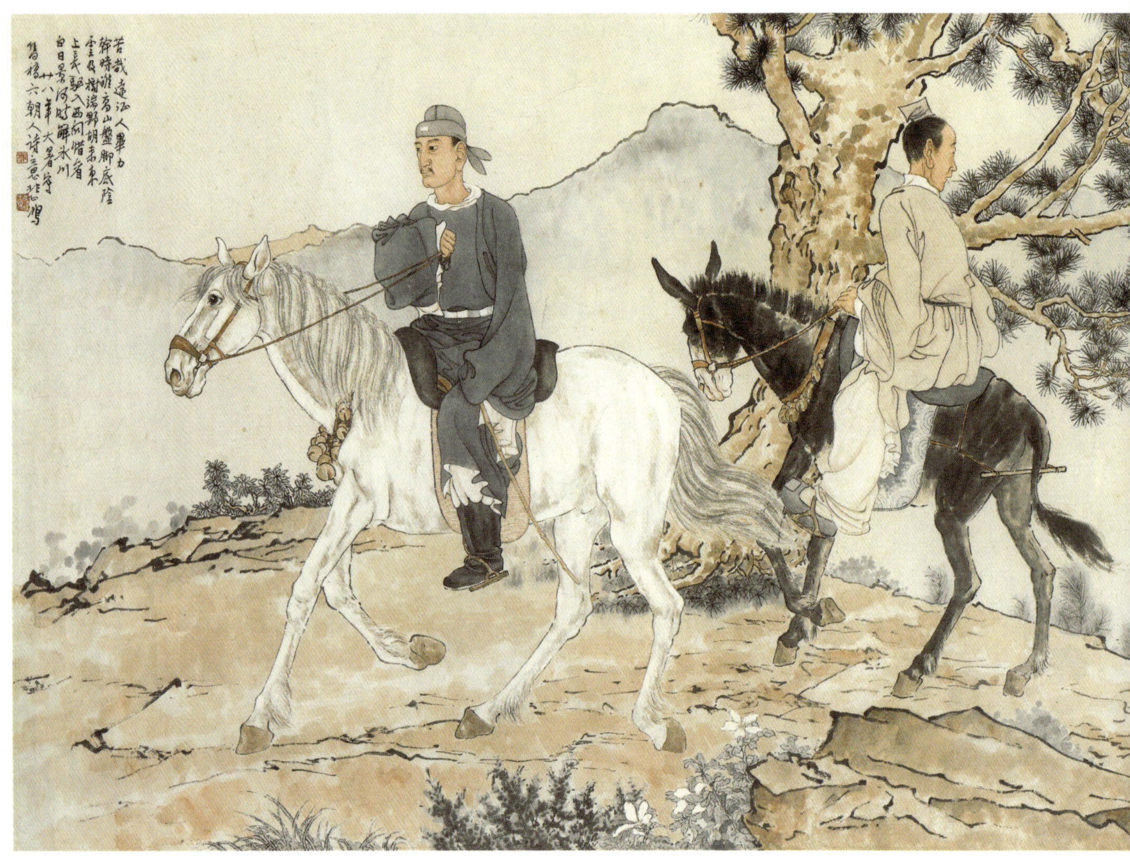

Xu Beihong
A Painting in the Spirit of Six Dynasties Poetry
1939
Chinese ink and colour on paper
102.5 × 206.2 cm
Collection of Nicky Yeo

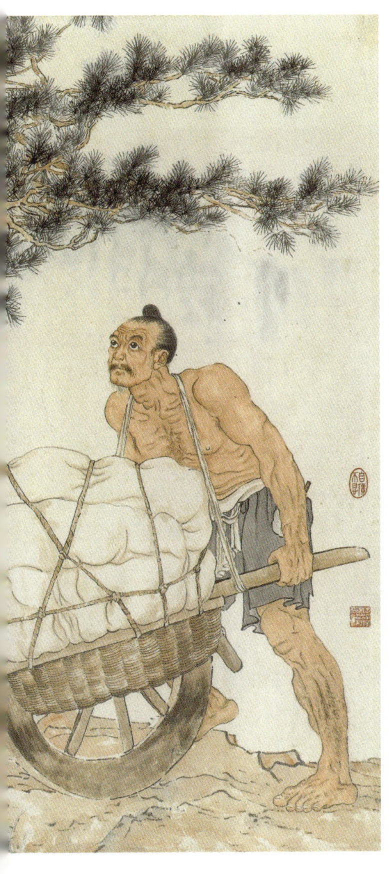

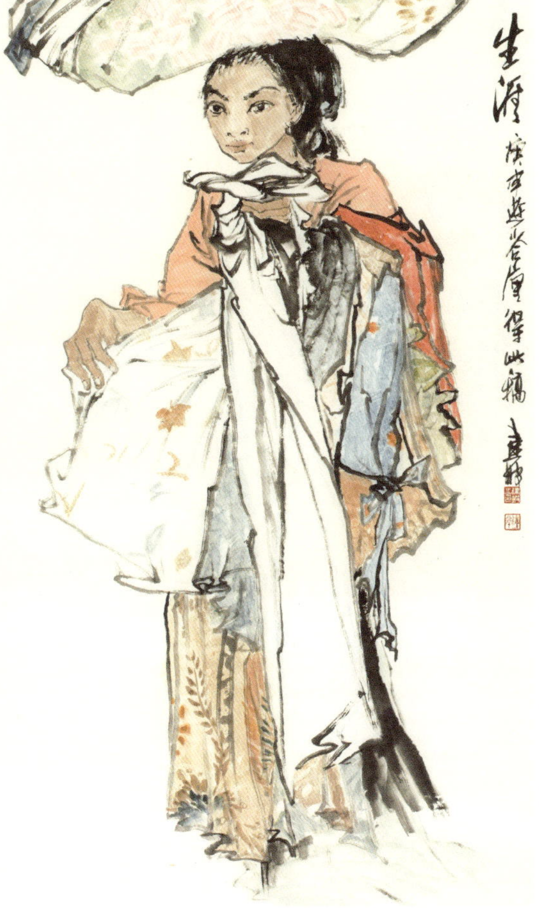

Tan Kian Por
Life
1982
Chinese ink and colour on paper
149 × 82 cm

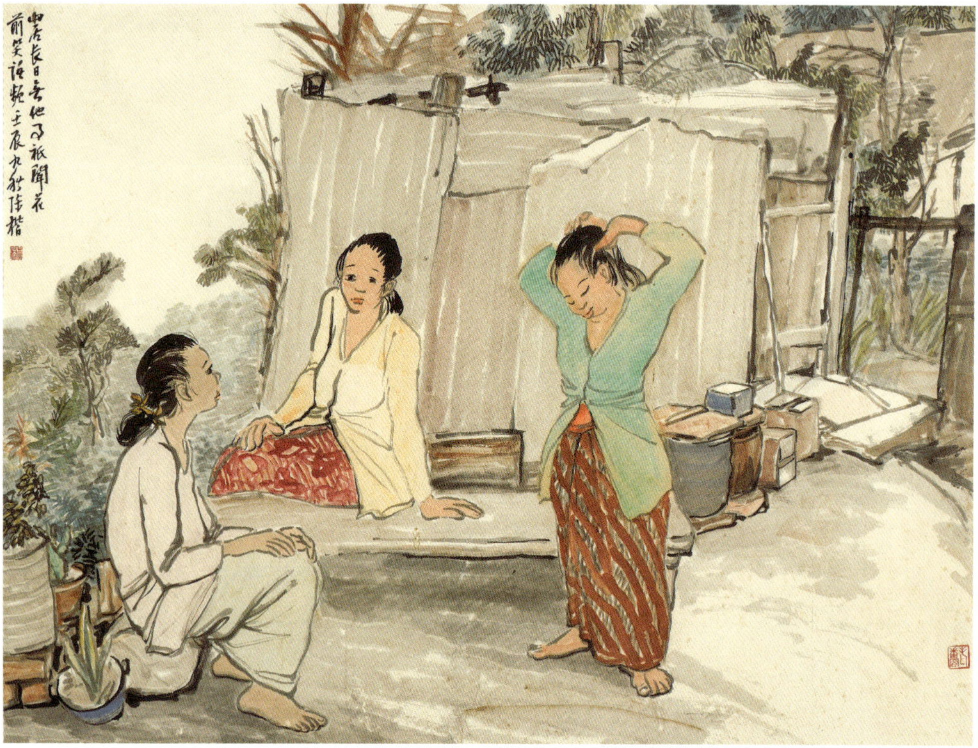

After Bath attests to Chen Chong Swee's mastery of Chinese ink techniques, which he employed to depict scenes from Southeast Asia. The bathers in this scene of calm idyll are succinctly fleshed out with the artist's traditional linear brushwork. The use of fixed-point perspective, which contributes to the emphasis on realistic depiction, represents a departure from the conventions of traditional Chinese painting.

Chen Chong Swee. *After Bath*. 1952. Chinese ink and colour on paper, 76 × 119 cm. Gift of the family of the late Chen Chong Swee.

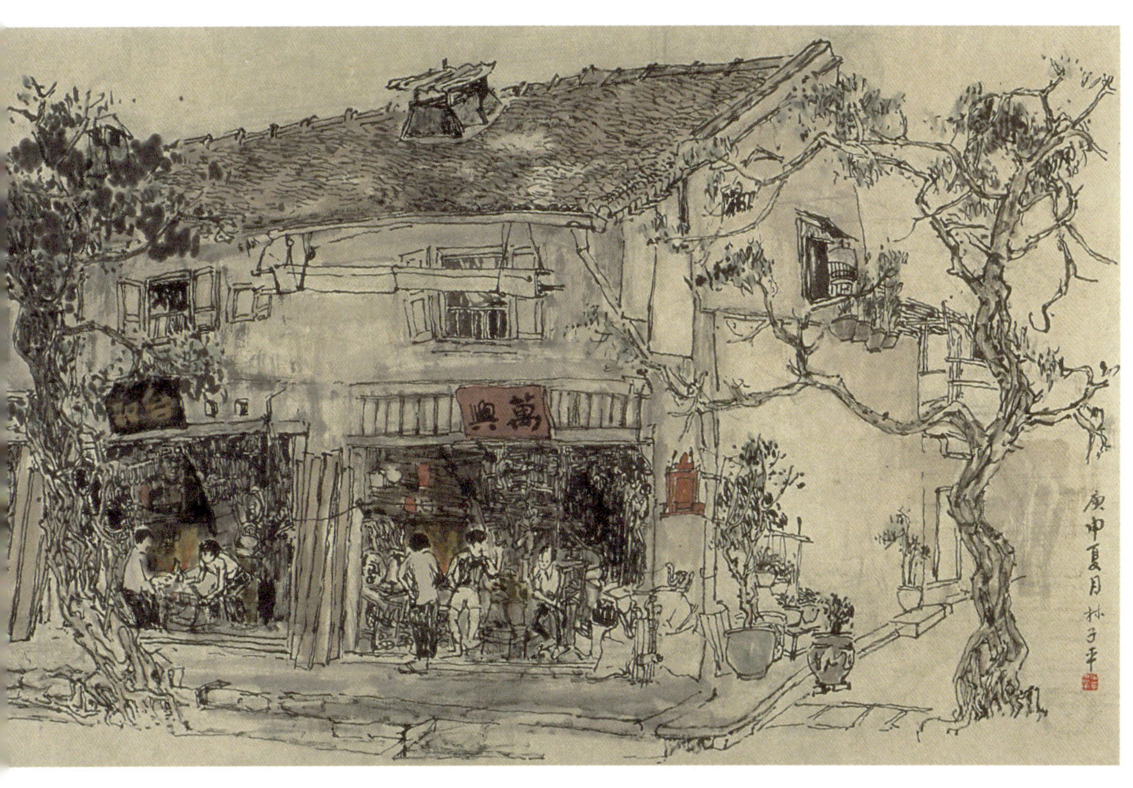

Lim Tze Peng
Blacksmith
1980
Ink and colour on paper
67 × 124 cm
Gift of Mobil Oil Singapore Pte Ltd

Henri Chen Kezhan
Self-Portrait I & Self-Portrait II
1989
Chinese ink and colour on paper
186 × 47 cm each

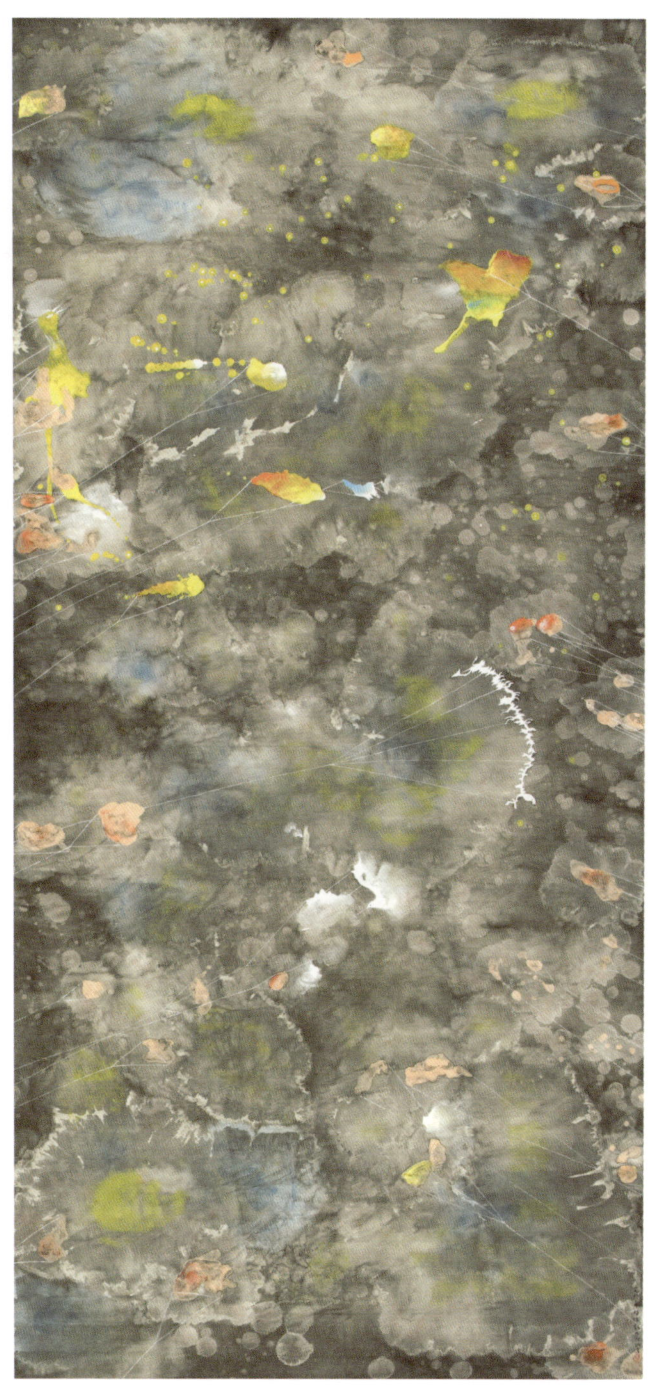

Tan Swie Hian
Night Kites
1988
Chinese ink and colour on paper
181 × 98 cm

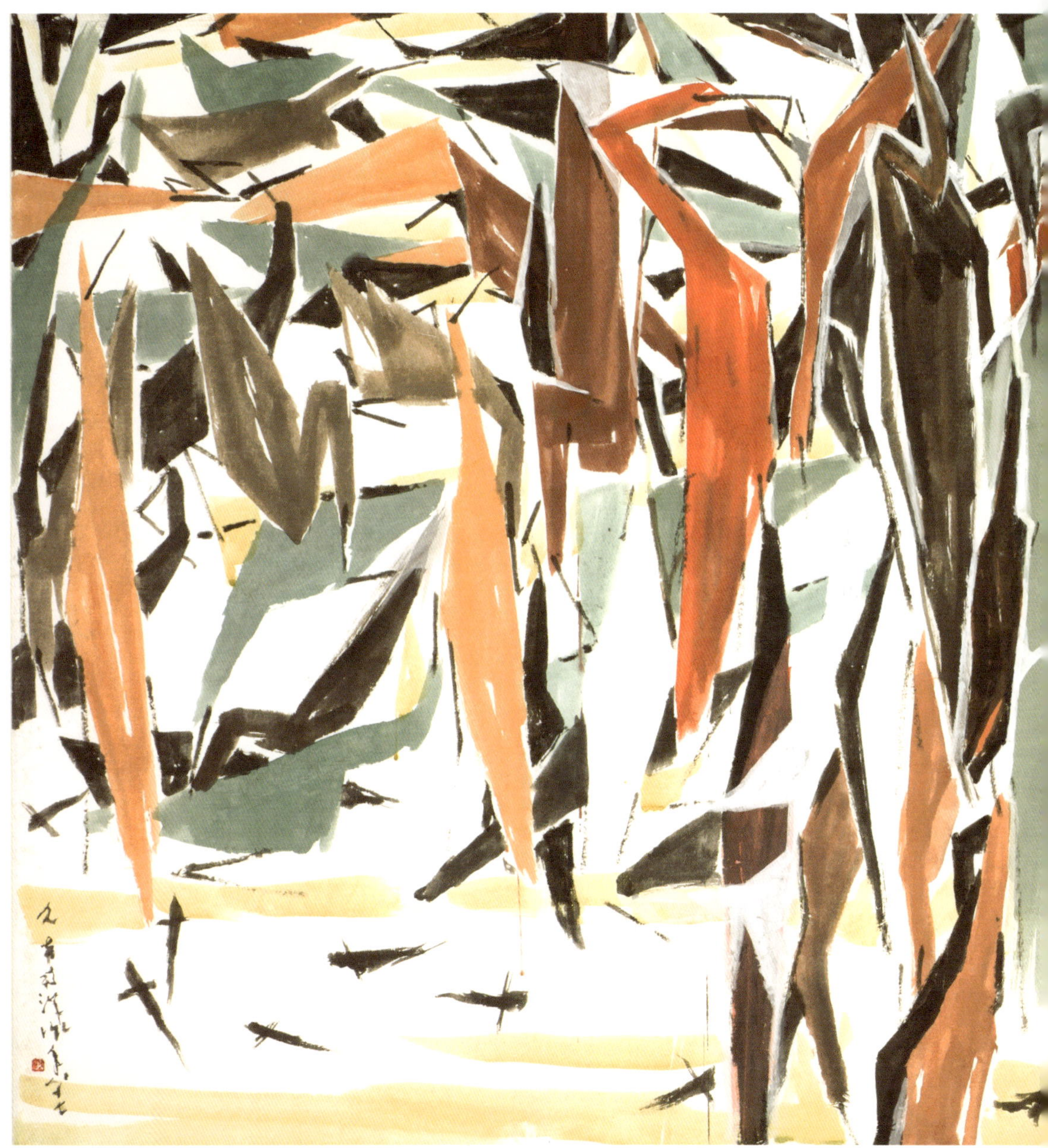

A dense picture, teeming with life, unfolds across this monumental work. It is a flock of herons, represented by interlocking and overlapping forms that push the picture towards abstraction. While informed by Cubism, Chen Wen Hsi was also rooted in the Chinese ink painting tradition. Although Herons was created near the end of Chen's life, its brushstrokes bear much vitality and spontaneity—two essential qualities of Chinese ink brushwork.

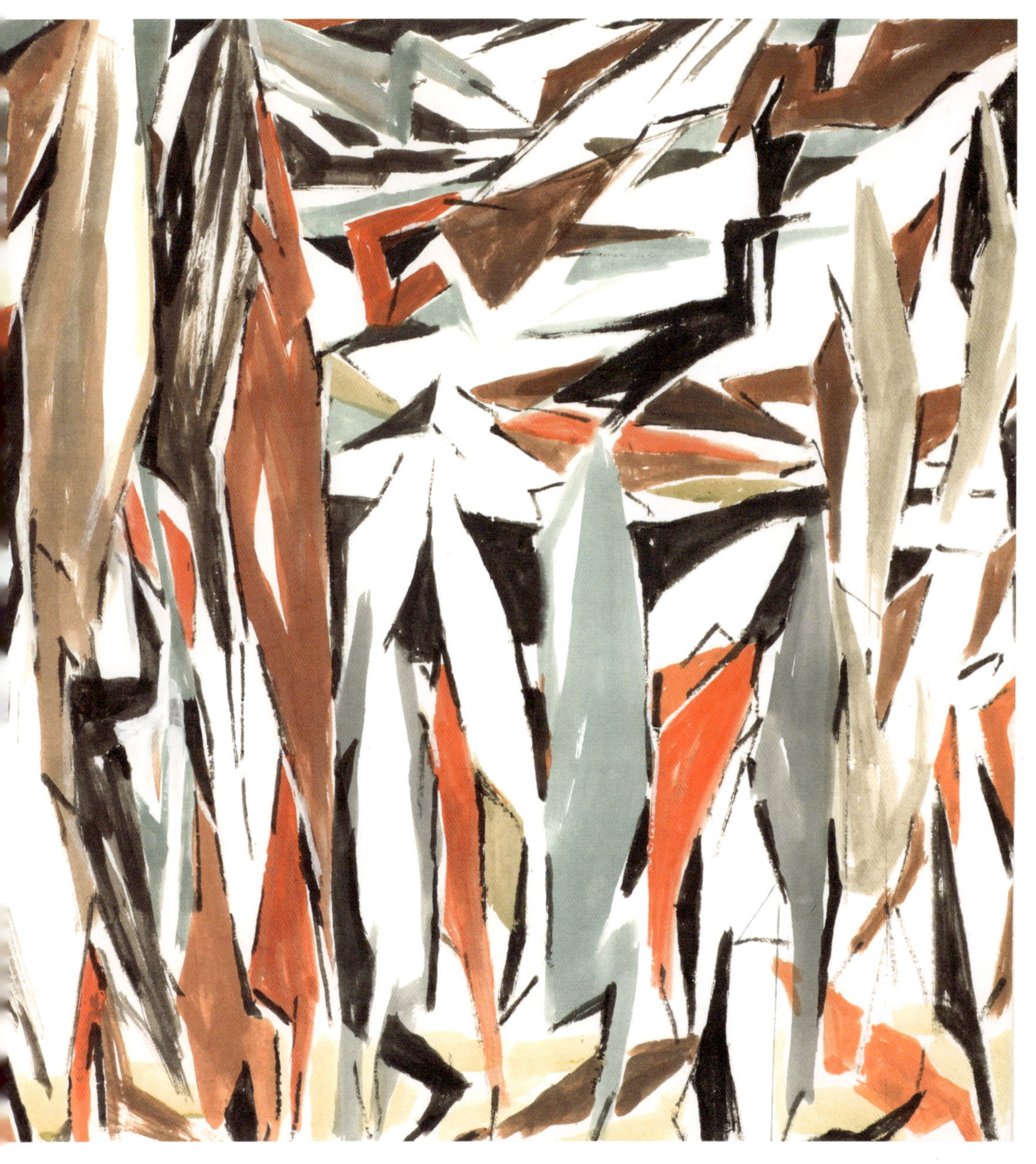

Chen Wen Hsi
Herons
c. 1991
Chinese ink and colour on paper, 123 × 245 cm
Collection of Singapore Art Museum

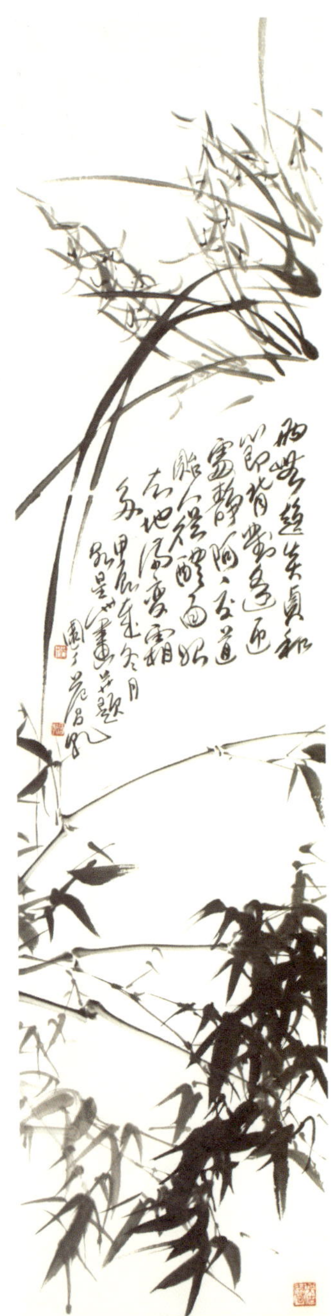

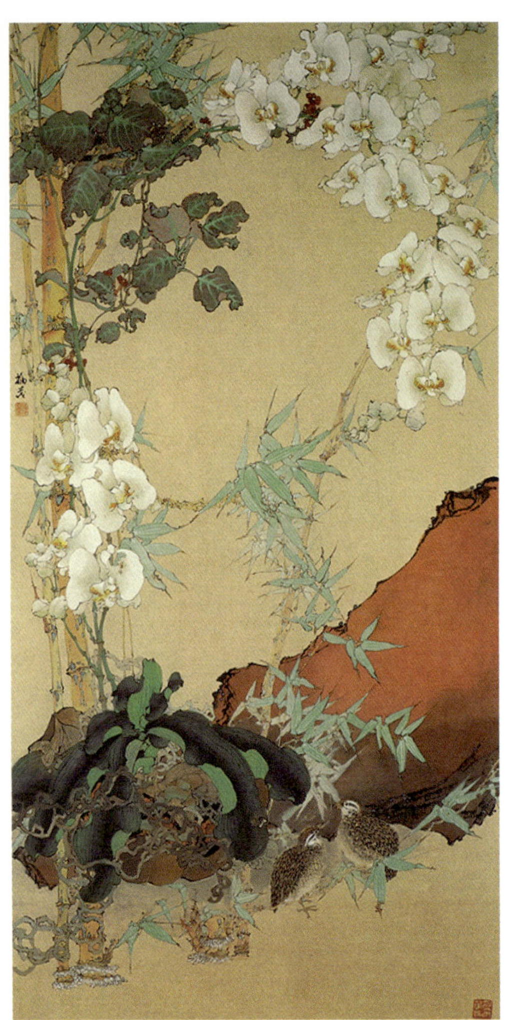

Lee Hock Moh
Flamboyance
1983
Chinese ink and colour on paper
132 × 67 cm

Fan Chang Tien
Bamboo
1964
Chinese ink on paper
145 × 35 cm
Gift of Heng Siew Leng

Chua Ek Kay
Yellow Door 1 & 2
1992
Chinese ink and colour on paper
184 × 100 cm each
Gift of the artist

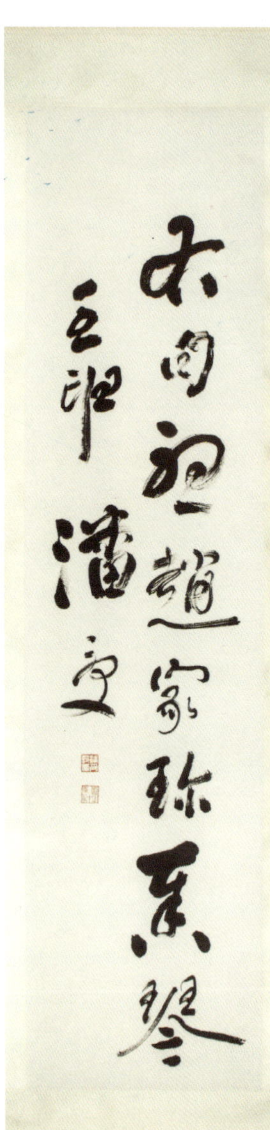

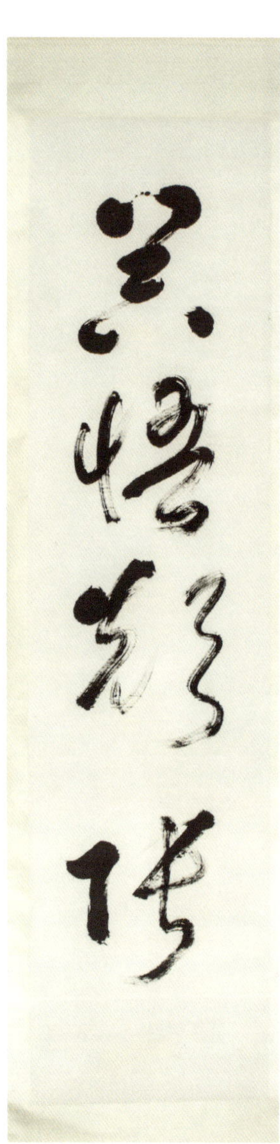

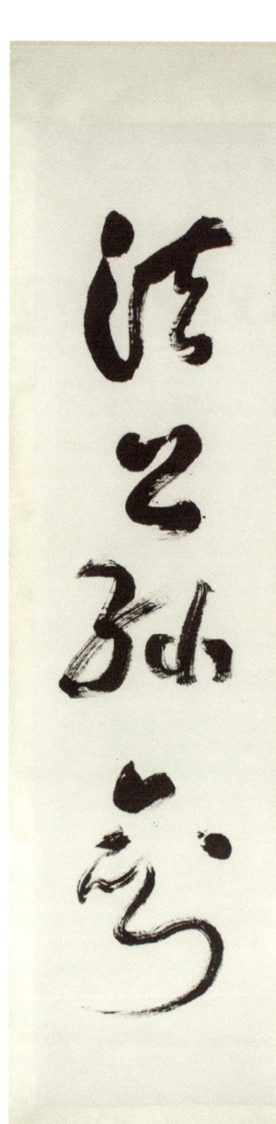

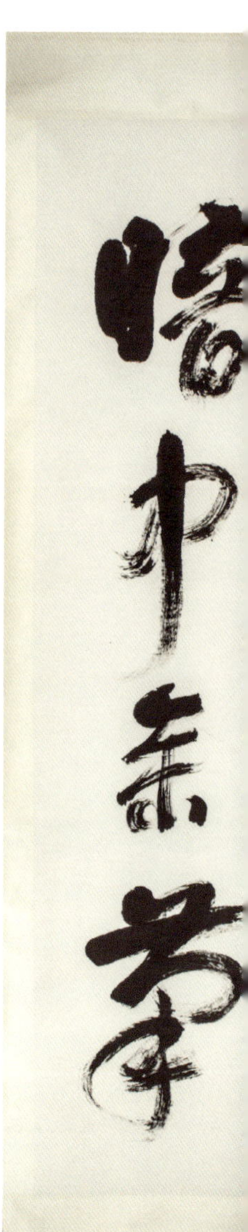

Pan Shou
Poem of Zither
1992
Chinese ink on paper
248 × 64 cm each
Collection of Singapore Art Museum

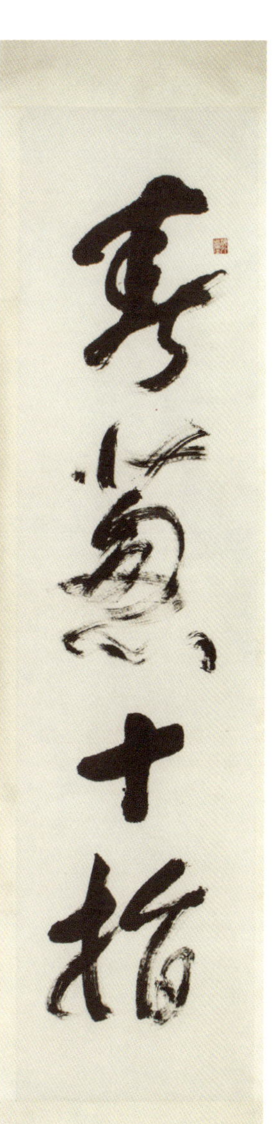

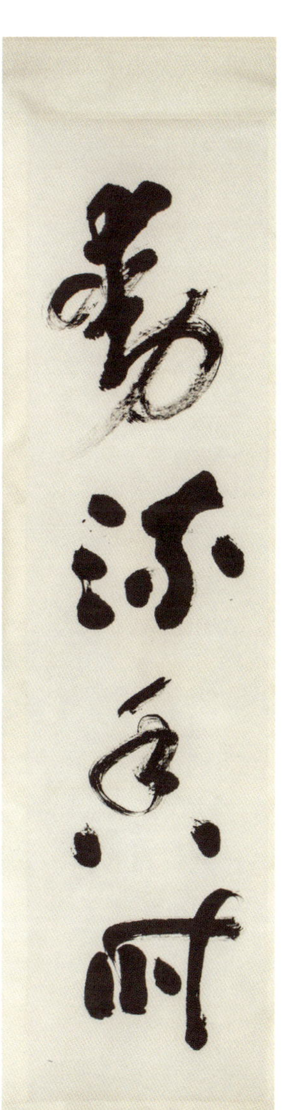

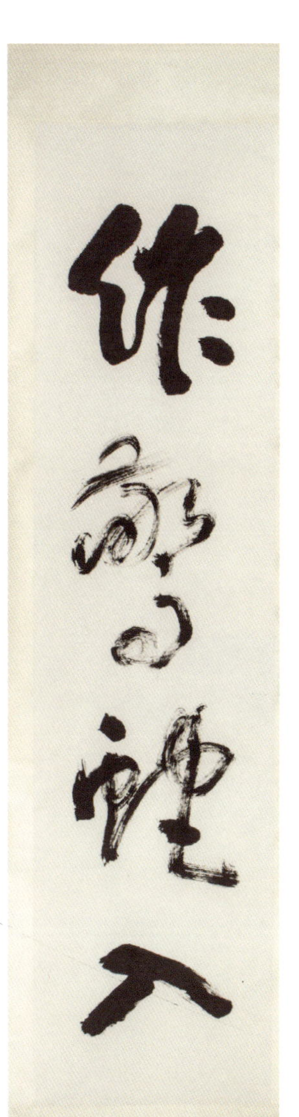

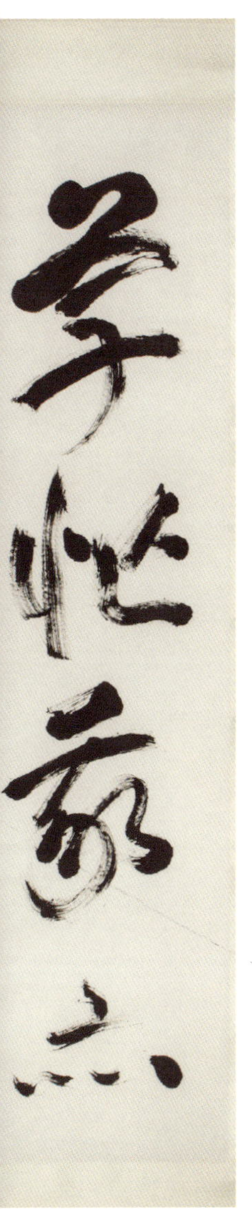

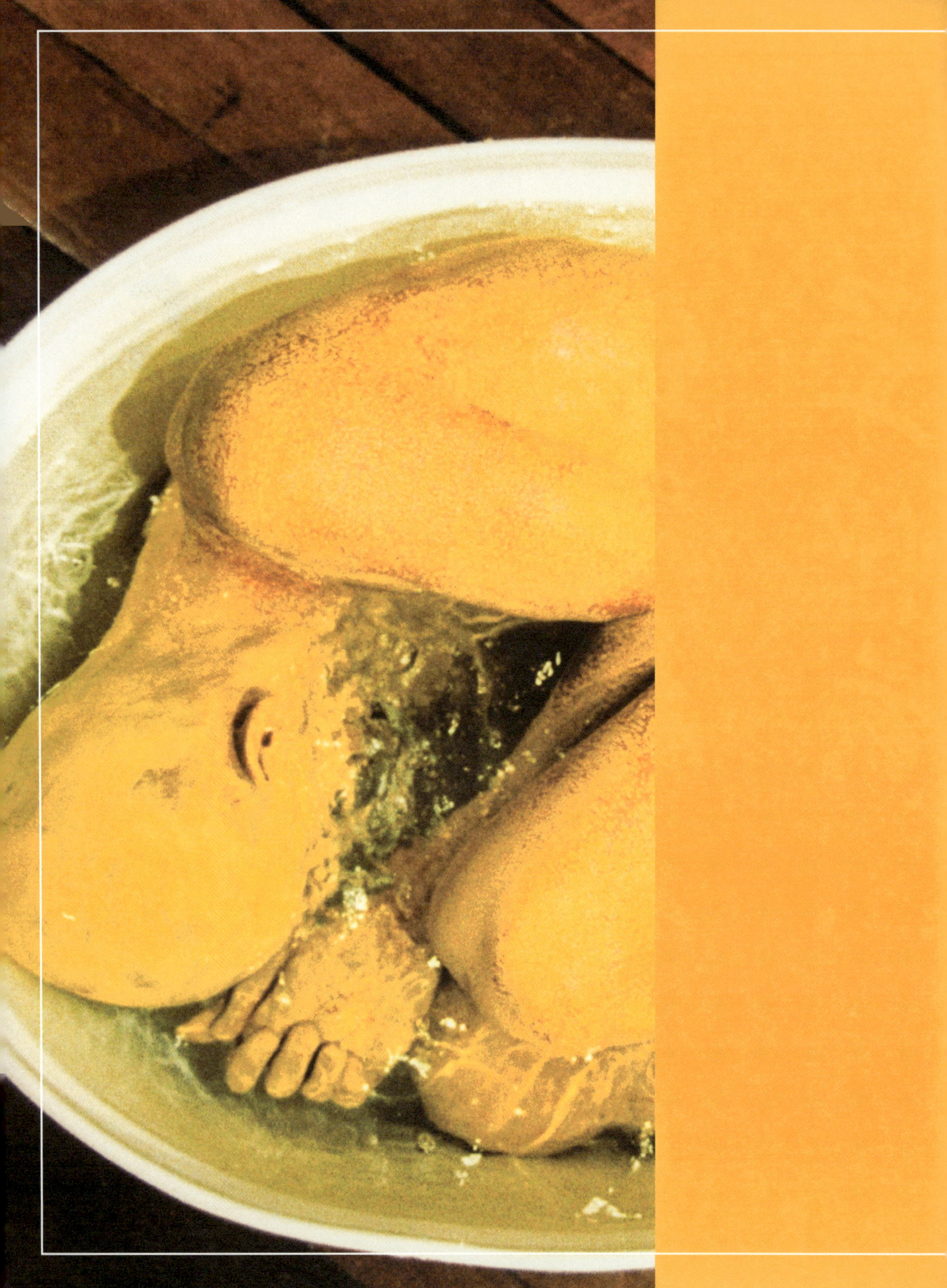

Shifting Grounds

"What is, or could be, art?" This question can be said to resonate with developments in the 1980s and 1990s. New approaches to art were manifested, as artists presented radical performances, scavenged materials and site-specific installations. Performances engaged audiences and signalled collaborative futures. Art freed itself from material forms to resist commodification, only to be archived, restaged and documented.

Amid these shifting frontiers, artists formed avant-garde collectives that operated at the fringes. An example is The Artists Village, a collective formed in the late 1980s that brought art to public spaces in response to the social concerns of the day. The spirit of independent experimentation that characterised the period is apparent in The Artists Village's manifesto, where it sets out its aim of establishing "an open space for artists."

Although these shifts in the production and consumption of art have precedents in the 1970s, they gained momentum in the 1980s and 1990s. As the art world turned away from traditional Euro-American centres of art towards the global, artists exhibited increasingly at international platforms, throwing issues of tradition and identity into relief.

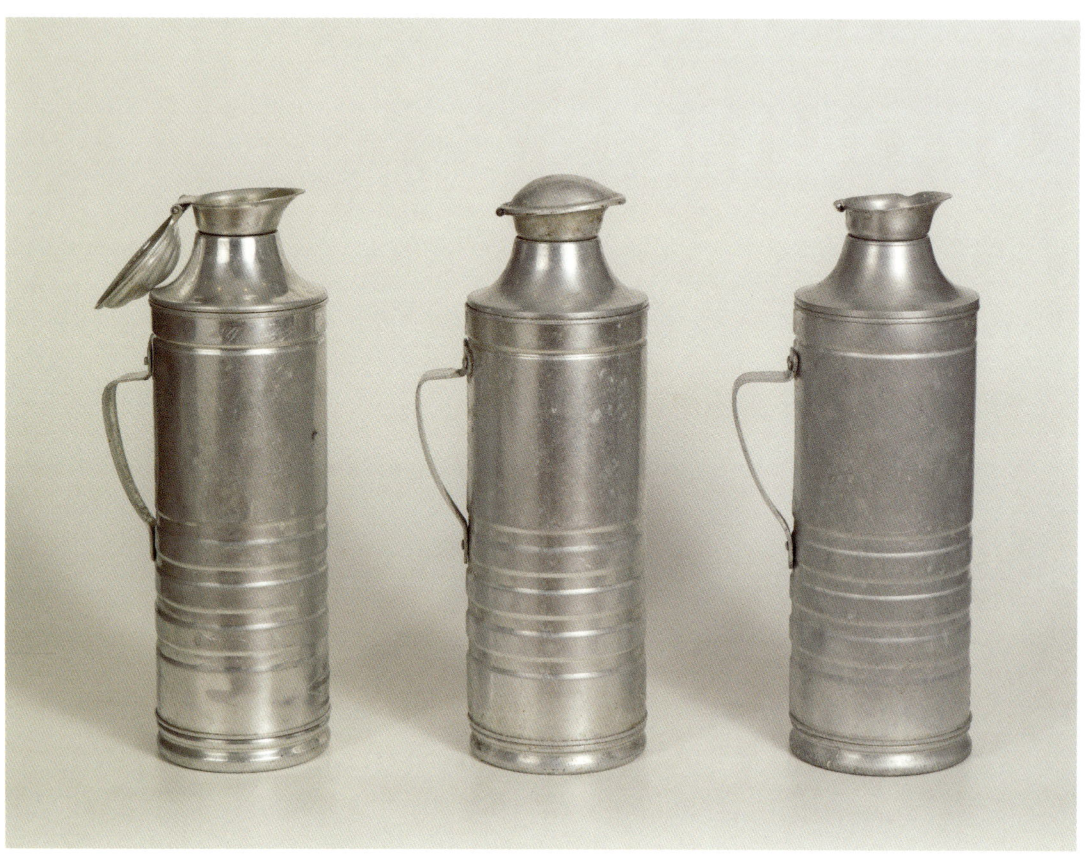

Faizal Fadil, a young member of The Artists Village, bought these flasks from the Sungei Road flea market and asserted them as a sculpture. By this simple gesture of the artist, these mass-produced everyday objects were transformed into art in a museum setting—an allusion to avant-garde artist Marcel Duchamp's concept of the readymade. This action was at the centre of a heated public debate: is this art?

M. Faizal Fadil. *Study of 3 Thermos Flasks*. 1991. Aluminium, 33 × 13.5 × 10.5 cm each. Collection of Singapore Art Museum.

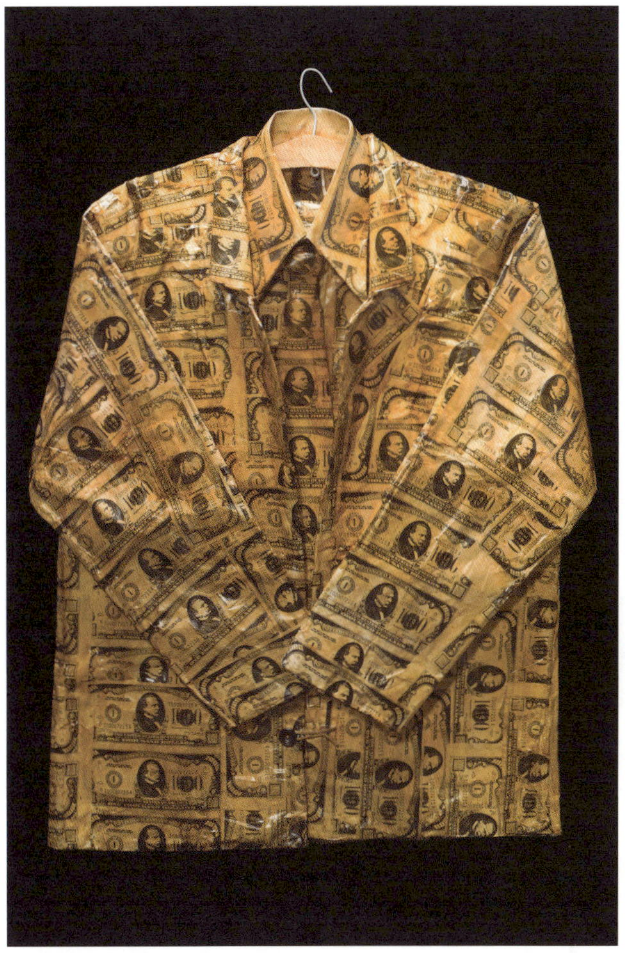

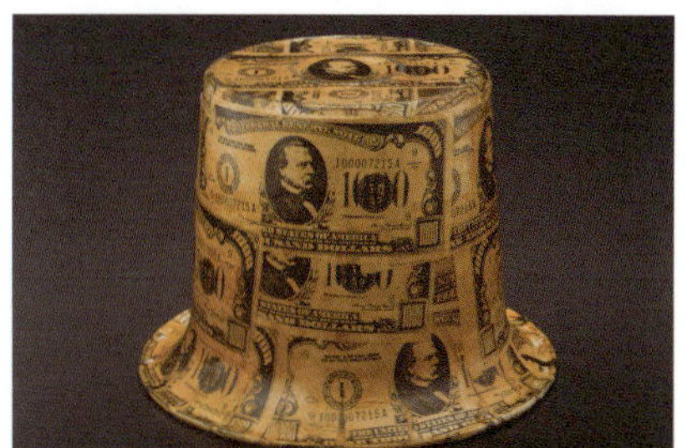

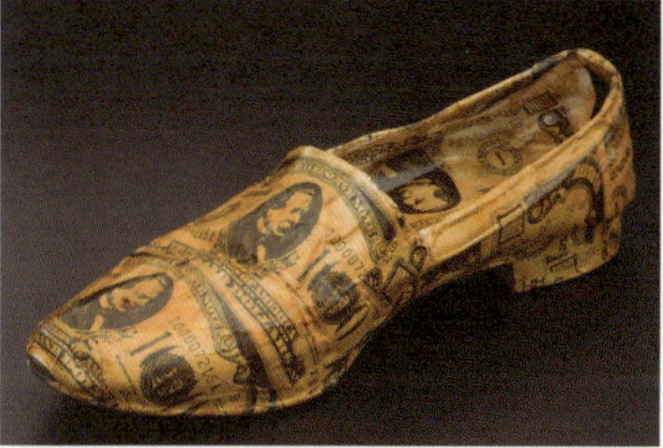

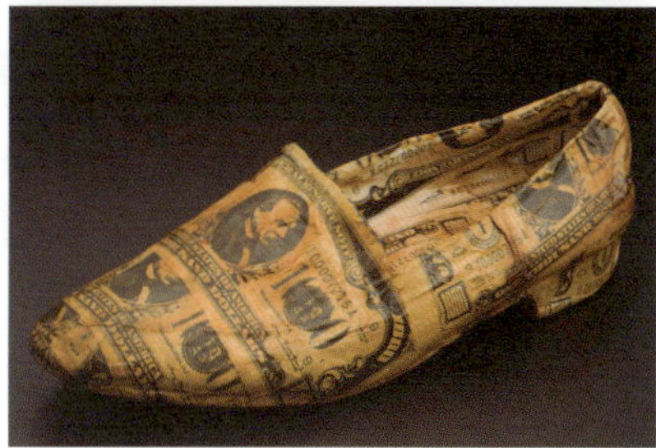

The stiffness of this suit belies its beginnings: it was worn by the artist in 1992, during a performance at Hong Bee Warehouse. Entitled *Lifestyles of the Rich and Famous: The Three-Legged Toad*, the performance was a critique of materialism and consumerism in Singapore. His mouth stuffed with fake American dollar bills, Vincent Leow leapt around in mimicry of the mythical three-legged toad, a symbol of wealth in Chinese geomancy.

Vincent Leow. *Money Suit*. 1992. Paper collage and cotton, dimensions variable. Collection of Singapore Art Museum.

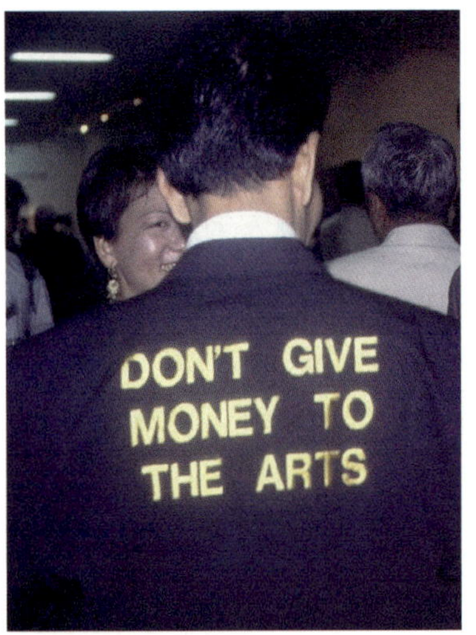

This is a relic from a performance by Tang Da Wu at the inauguration of a major arts festival in 1995, involving then President Ong Teng Cheong. Tang asked for the president's permission to don this jacket before presenting him with a letter that read, "I am an artist. I am important." This is one of Tang's most iconic works that engages with issues confronting the practice of art in Singapore.

Tang Da Wu. *Don't Give Money to the Arts*. 1995. Mixed media, dimensions variable.

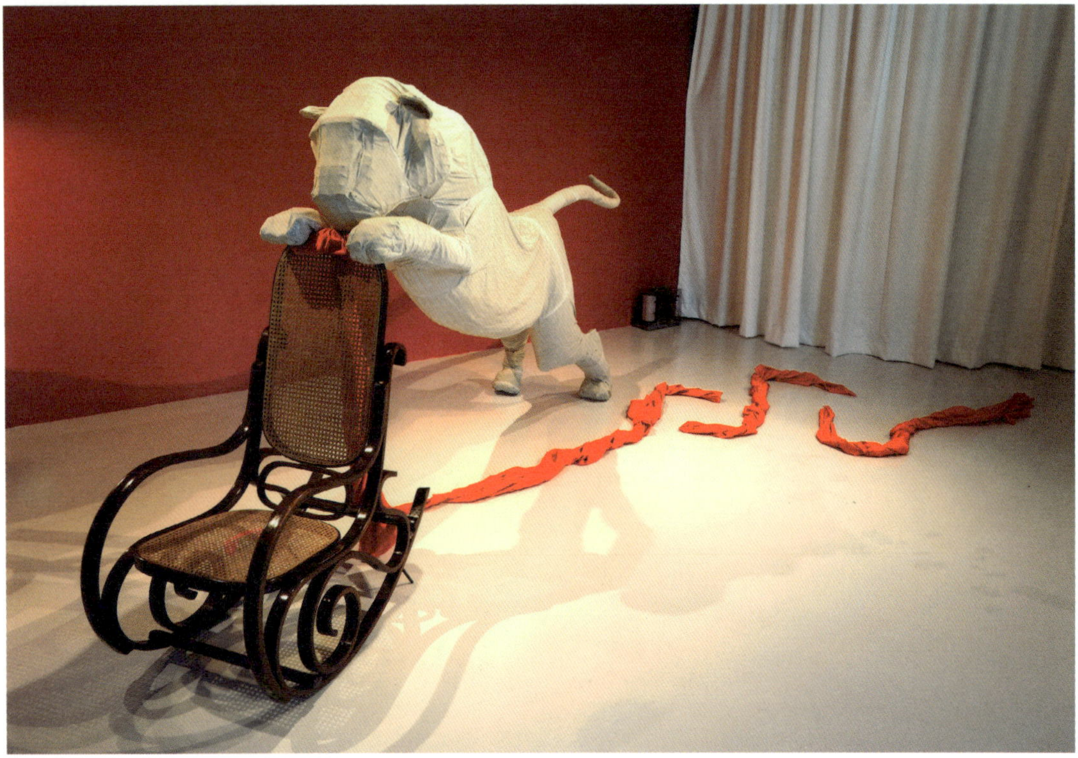

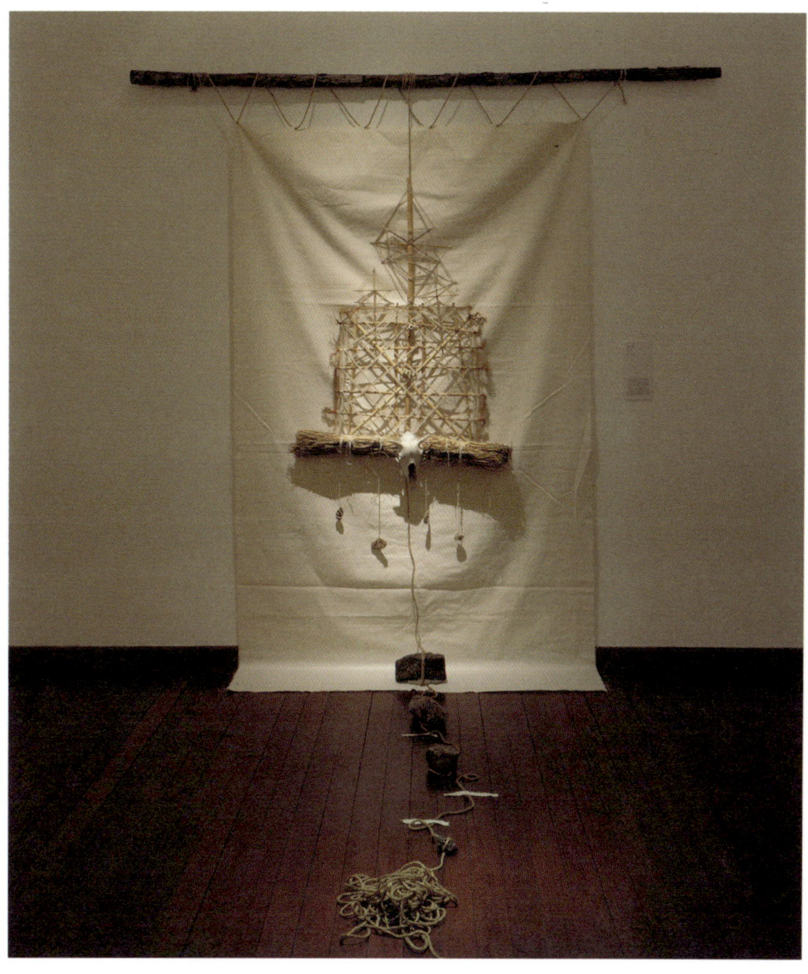

Salleh Japar
Spirit Trap
1989
Mixed media
Dimensions variable

OPPOSITE PAGE

Performance, installation or sculpture? A critical response to tiger poaching in Asia, Tiger's Whip was staged in 1991 as an installation with ten tigers and a large wooden bed, with Tang Da Wu performing as poacher, tiger and consumer. Later that year, Tang used one tiger for a workshop at the Sculpture Seminar, which resulted in the version shown here. Tiger's Whip established Tang as a forerunner in challenging the conventional definitions of art.

Tang Da Wu and participants of *A Sculpture Seminar. Tiger's Whip* (also known as *I Want My Penis Back*). 1991. Mixed media, dimensions variable. Collection of Singapore Art Museum.

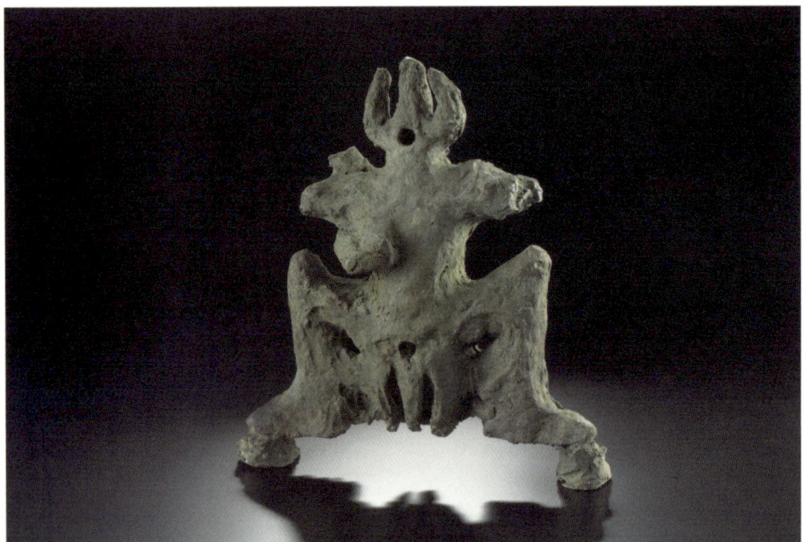

Despite its title, this work is not a traditional representation of a Hindu deity. Although S. Chadrasekaran was familiar with conventional depictions of *deva* because his family manufactured religious shrines, he invented a new artistic vocabulary based on his identity as an artist in Southeast Asia. In the Deva series of bronze sculptures, he expresses his ideas about man and animals with a primitive monumentality.

S. Chandrasekaran. *Deva Series III*. 1994. Bronze, 28.5 × 26.5 × 9.5 cm. Collection of Singapore Art Museum.

Word is dominated by bold triangles, yet a closer look reveals lines that radiate from the centre. Goh Ee Choo juxtaposes the formal shape of the triangle with the more organic pattern that fills it to create a symmetrical composition. Balance and energy are central to Goh's works, informed by his belief in Buddhism and *feng shui*. He wrote, "The importance of this work lies in the seeking of liberation within restriction."

Goh Ee Choo. *Word*. 1991. Pigment ink on paper, 113 × 153 cm. Collection of Singapore Art Museum.

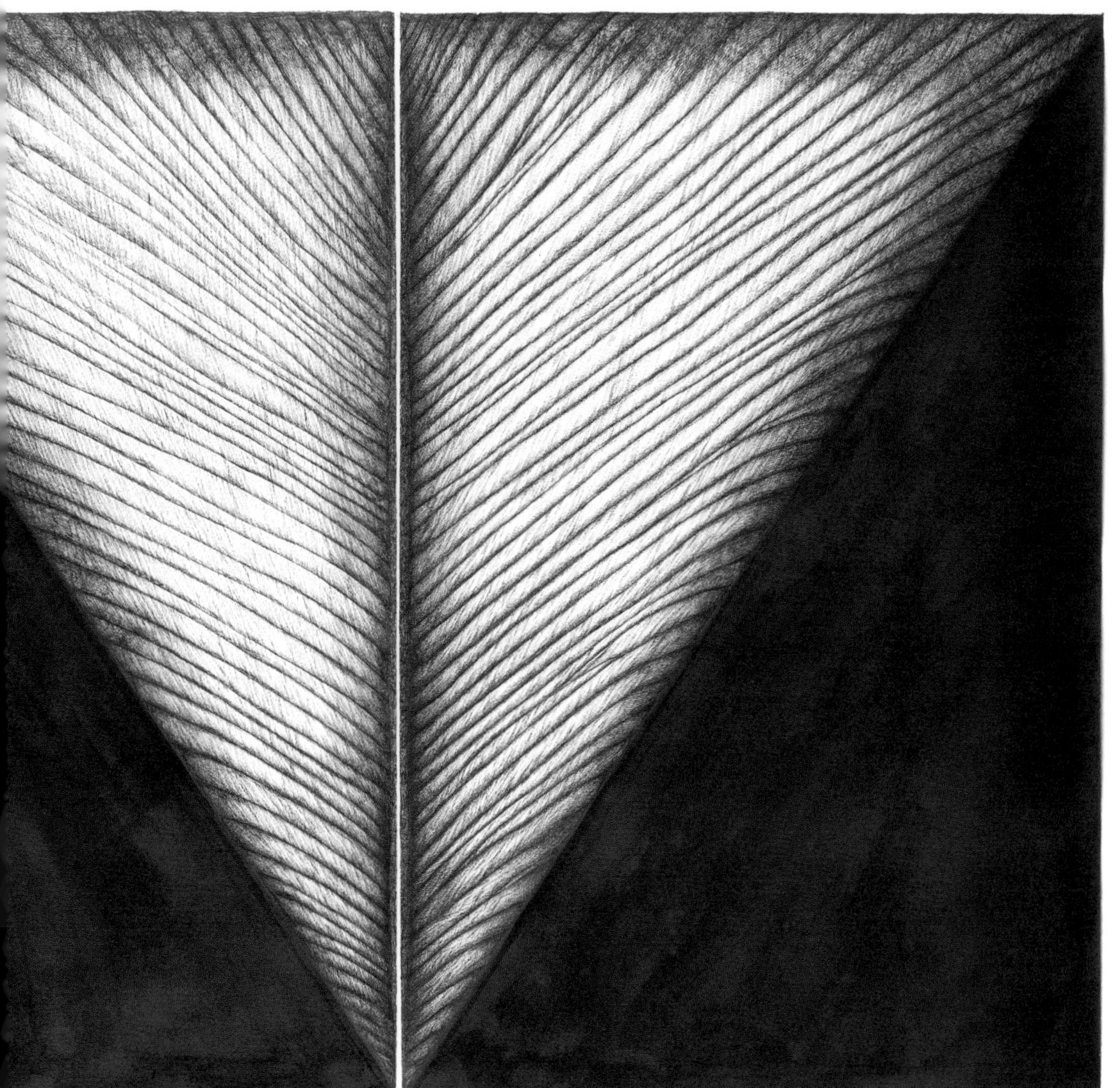

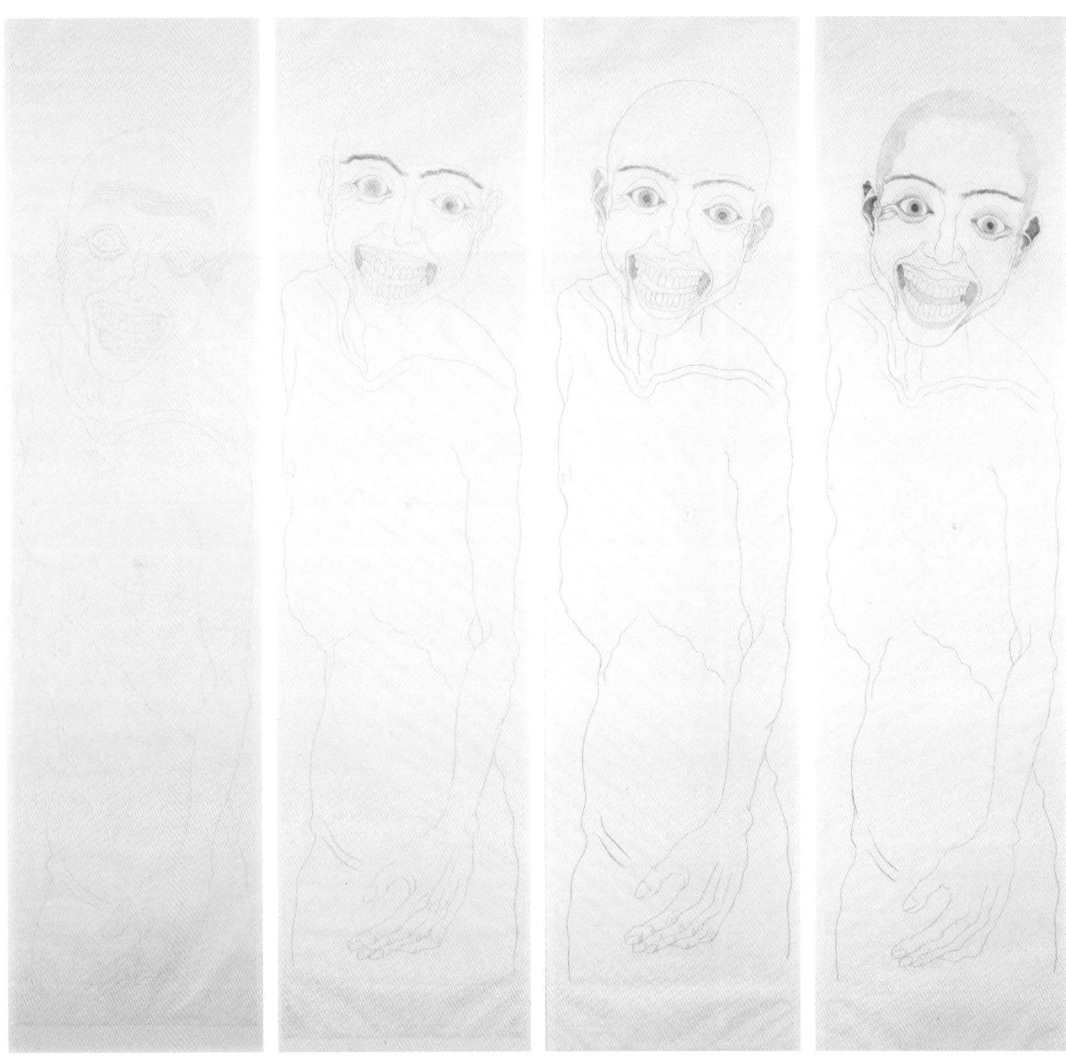

In 1994, the Singapore government withdrew funding for performance art. In response, Zai Kuning produced a series of repetitive and oversized self-portraits that grimace at the viewer. The title of this work is a clever play on words: a performance has been stilled, but will still continue nonetheless. Similarly, while the body in each portrait is stationary, together they create a sense of continuity, constituting a different kind of performance.

Zai Kuning. *Still Performance.* 1994. Pencil and watercolour on paper, 250.5 × 488 cm. Collection of Singapore Art Museum.

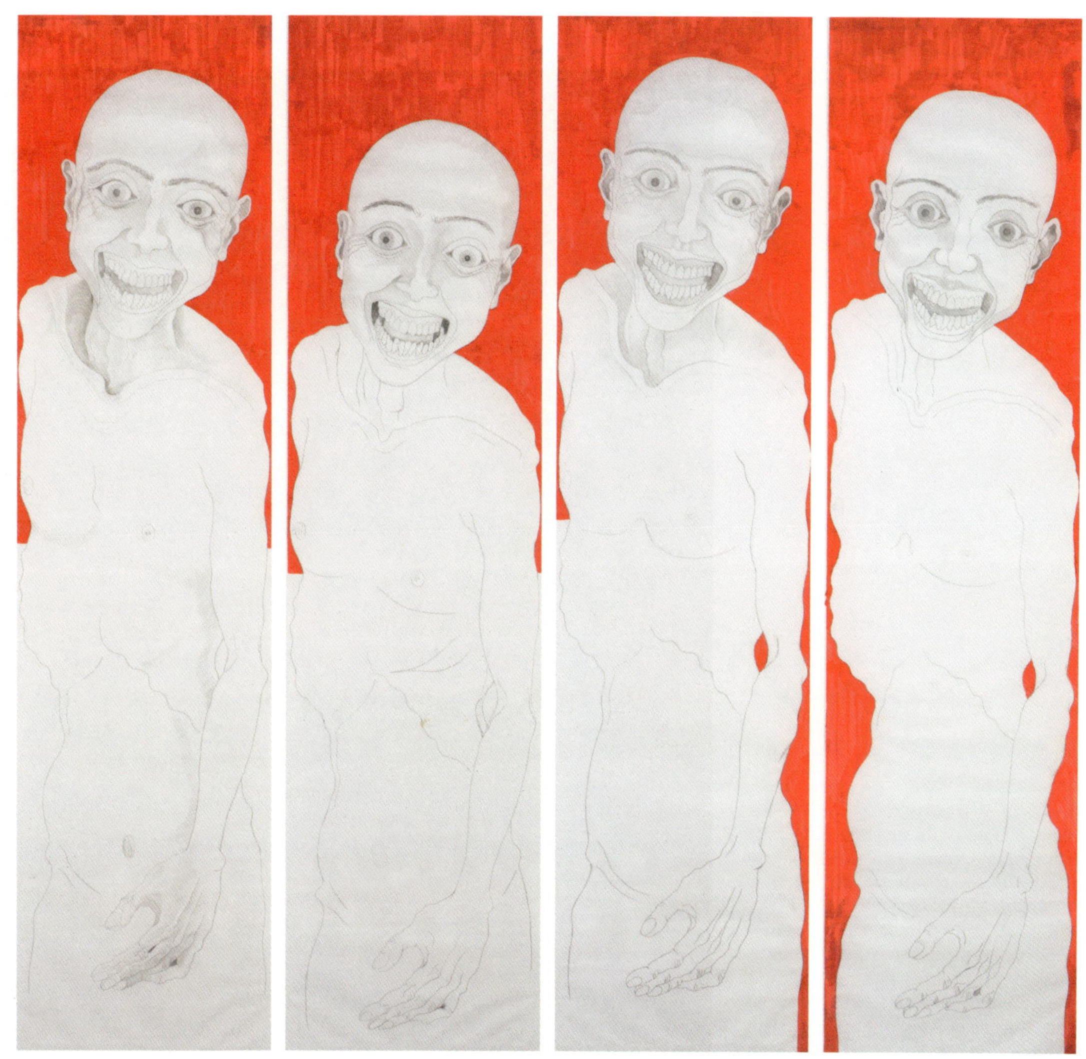

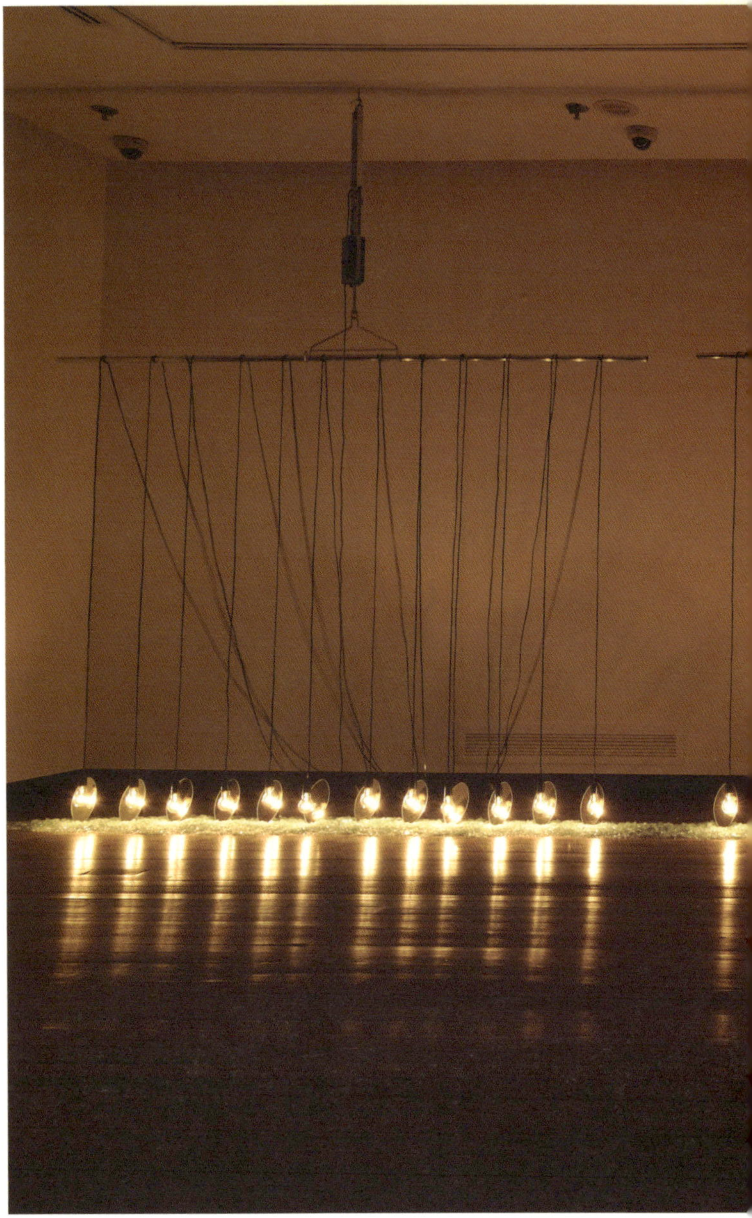

Rows of light bulbs suspended from an aluminium frame slip continuously against a row of mirrors, setting off a chorus of clinks. Over and over, the bulbs rub against their reflections in a cycle of unfulfilled narcissistic desire. Suzann Victor uses light, sound and movement in this installation to evoke the presence of a performing body. She made this work following a funding ban on performance art in Singapore in 1994.

Suzann Victor. *Expense of Spirit in a Waste of Shame*. 1994. Light bulbs, cables, control unit, broken glass, motors, aluminium rods and mirrors, dimensions variable. Collection of Singapore Art Museum.

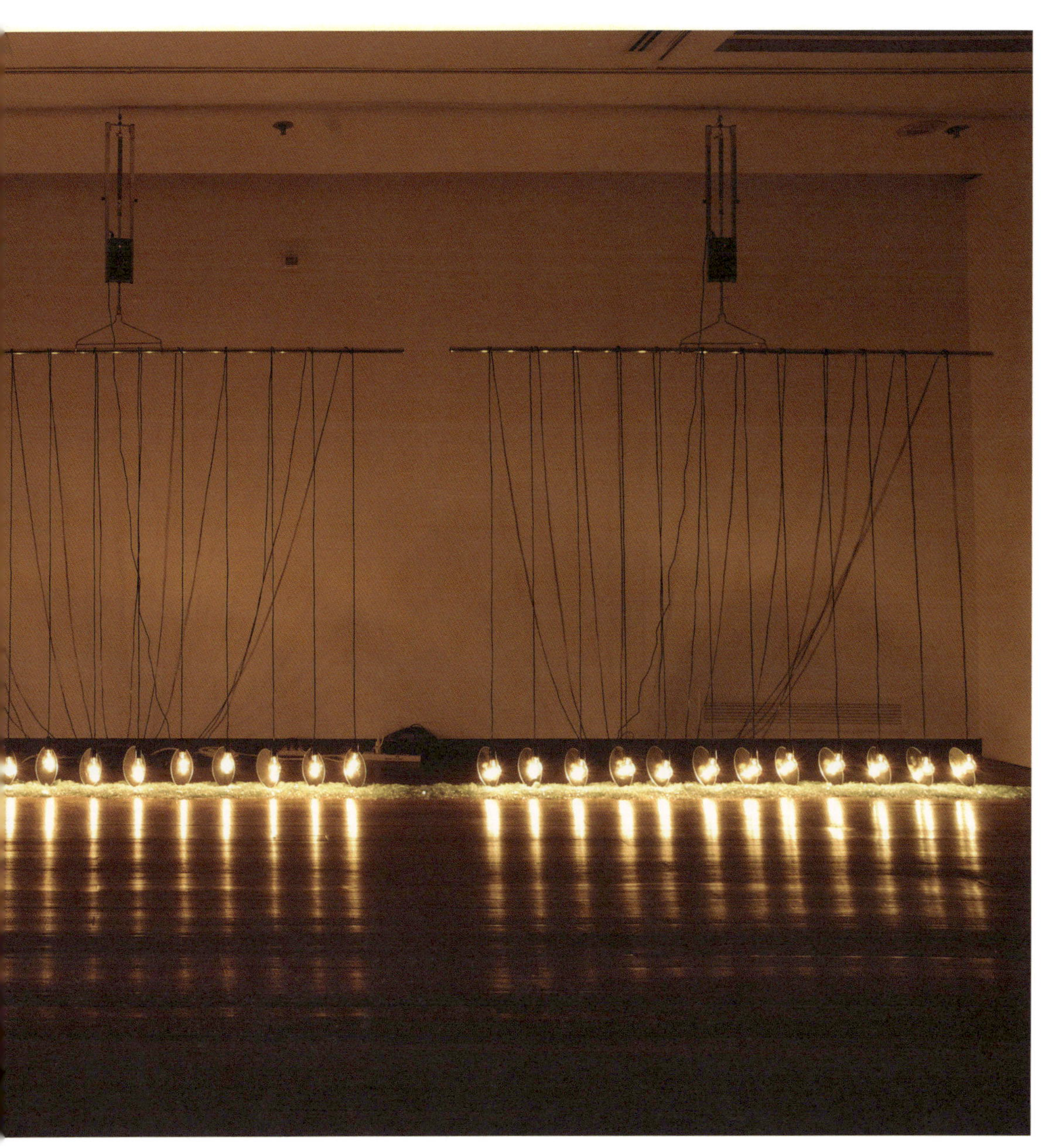

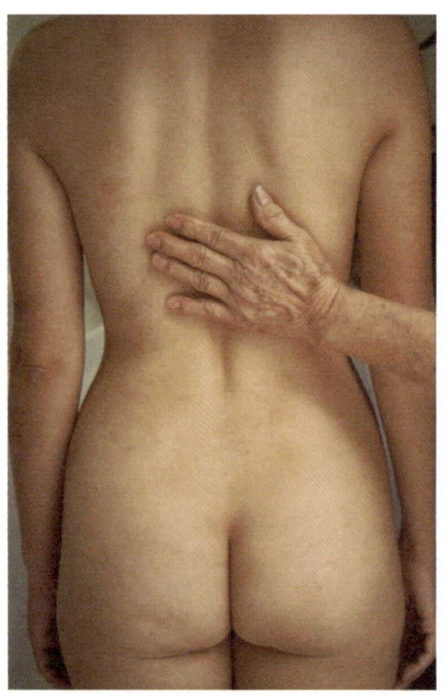

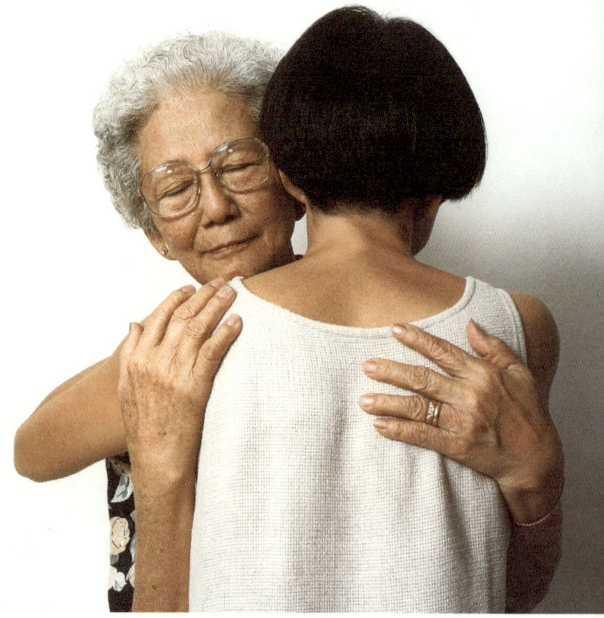

Another Woman features the artist Amanda Heng and her mother, their bodies informing an exploration of the relationship between mother and daughter, as well as the position of women in an Asian society. Heng was an early member of The Artists Village and one of the first artists in Singapore to comment on and investigate gender issues through performance.

Amanda Heng Liang Ngim. *Another Woman*. 1996–1997. Starched clothes, C-Print, L–R: 75 × 50 cm; 75.5 × 101 cm; 100.5 × 126 cm. Collection of Singapore Art Museum.

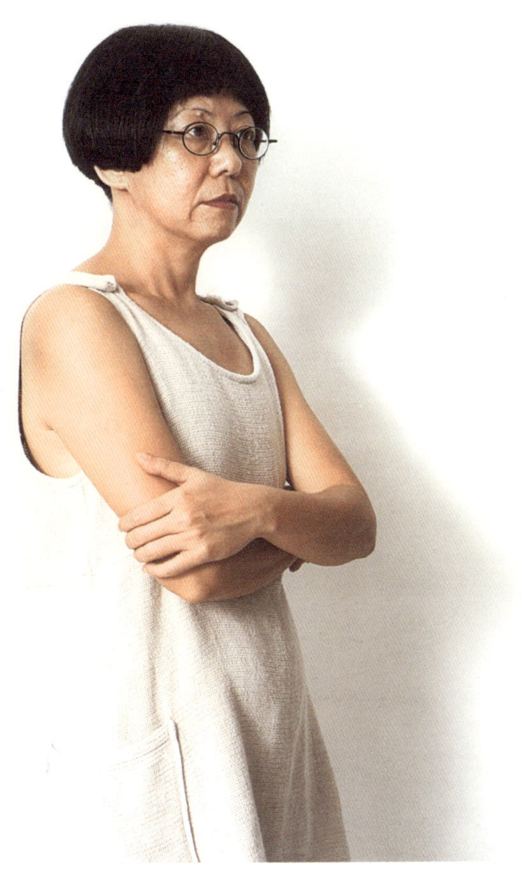

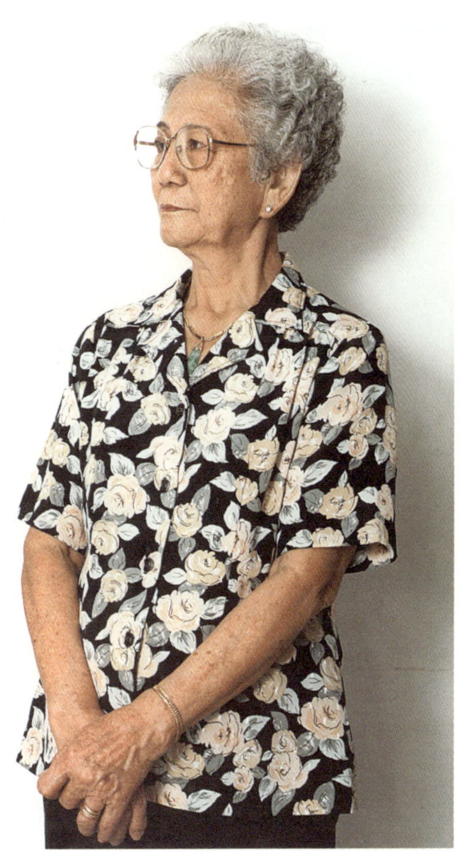

Since 1992, Lee Wen has appeared as the Yellow Man in a series of performances around the world. This particular performance took place at The Substation in 1997, where the artist presented a lecture before immersing himself in a tub to wash the yellow paint off his body. The performance critiqued an exhibition, *Singapore Art '97*, for over-representing ink and watercolour to the detriment of performance and installation art.

Lee Wen. *Journey of A Yellow Man No. 11: Multi-Culturalism.* 1997. Digital giclee print, 101.6 × 144.8 cm.

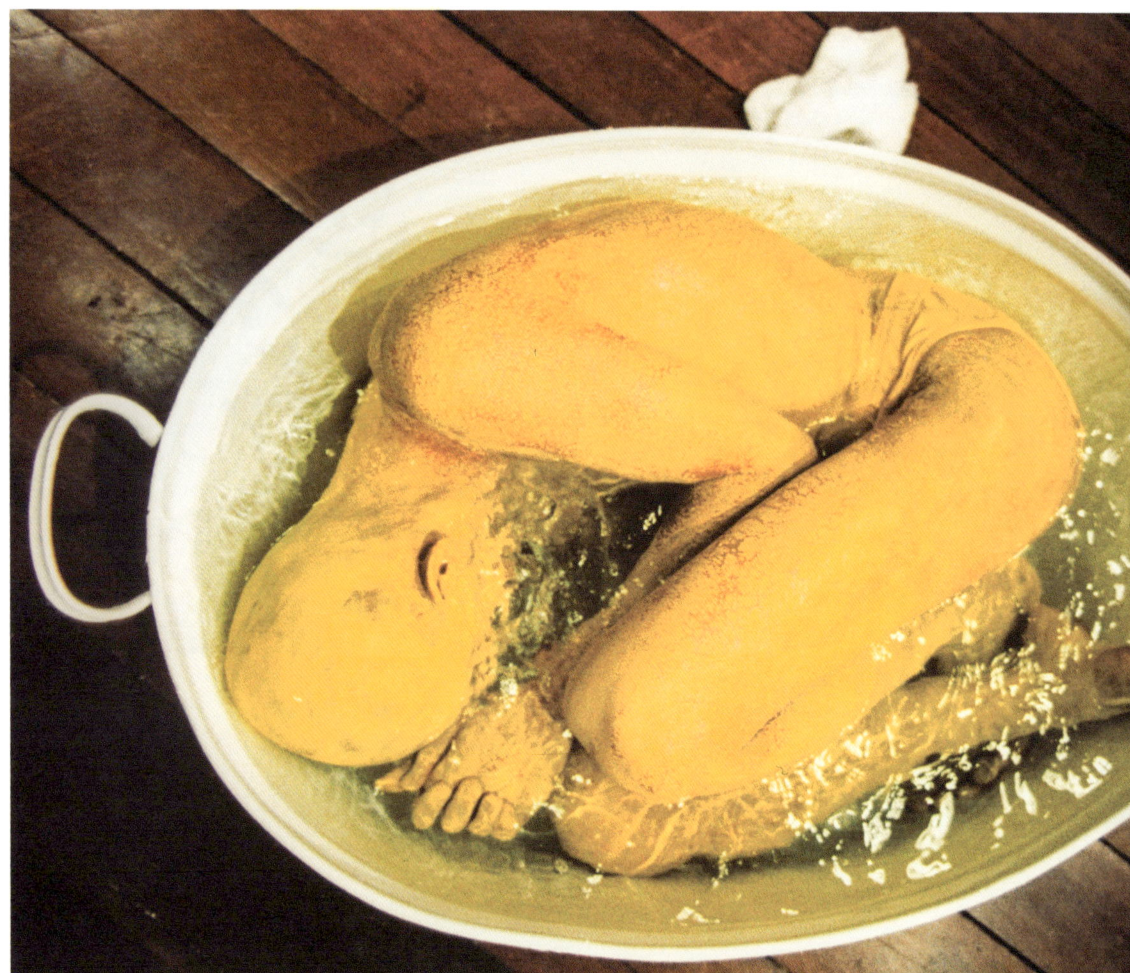

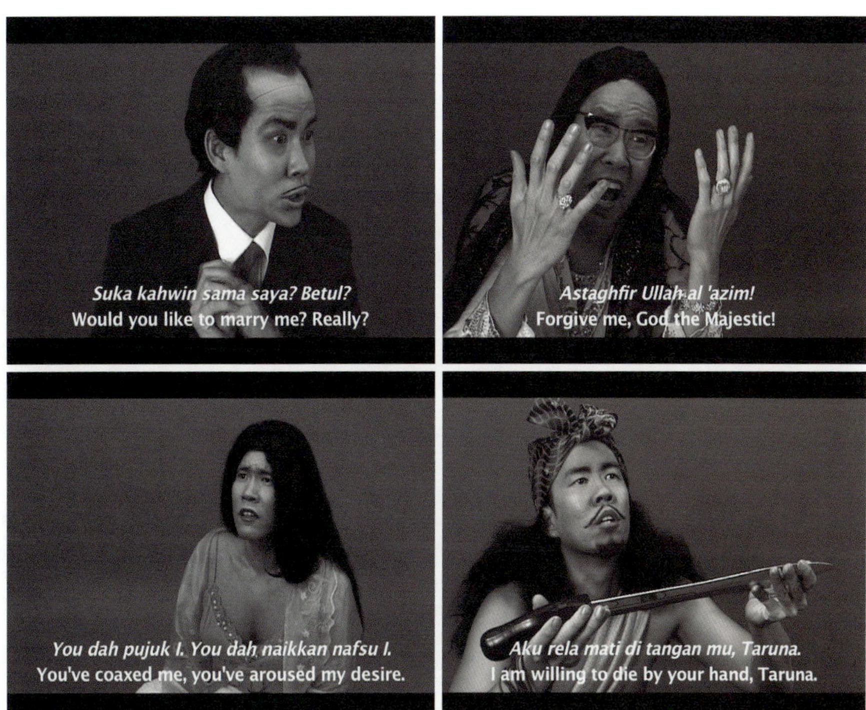

Four Malay Stories restages key scenes from four films made by actor-director P. Ramlee during the heyday of Singapore cinema, between the 1950s and 1970s. Ming Wong plays 16 characters, including an adulterous doctor, a downtrodden musician and an overbearing matriarch, parroting their lines and imitating their gestures. By taking on these disparate roles, Wong challenges our implicit assumptions about the connections between language, race and culture.

Ming Wong. *Four Malay Stories*. 2005. Four channel video installation, various durations (*Dr. Rushdi* 26:41, *Ibu Mertuaku* 26:48, *Labu dan Labi* 22:34, *Semerah Padi* 29:18). Collection of the artist. Image courtesy of the artist. Vitamin Creative Space, Guangzhou and carlier | gebauer, Berlin.

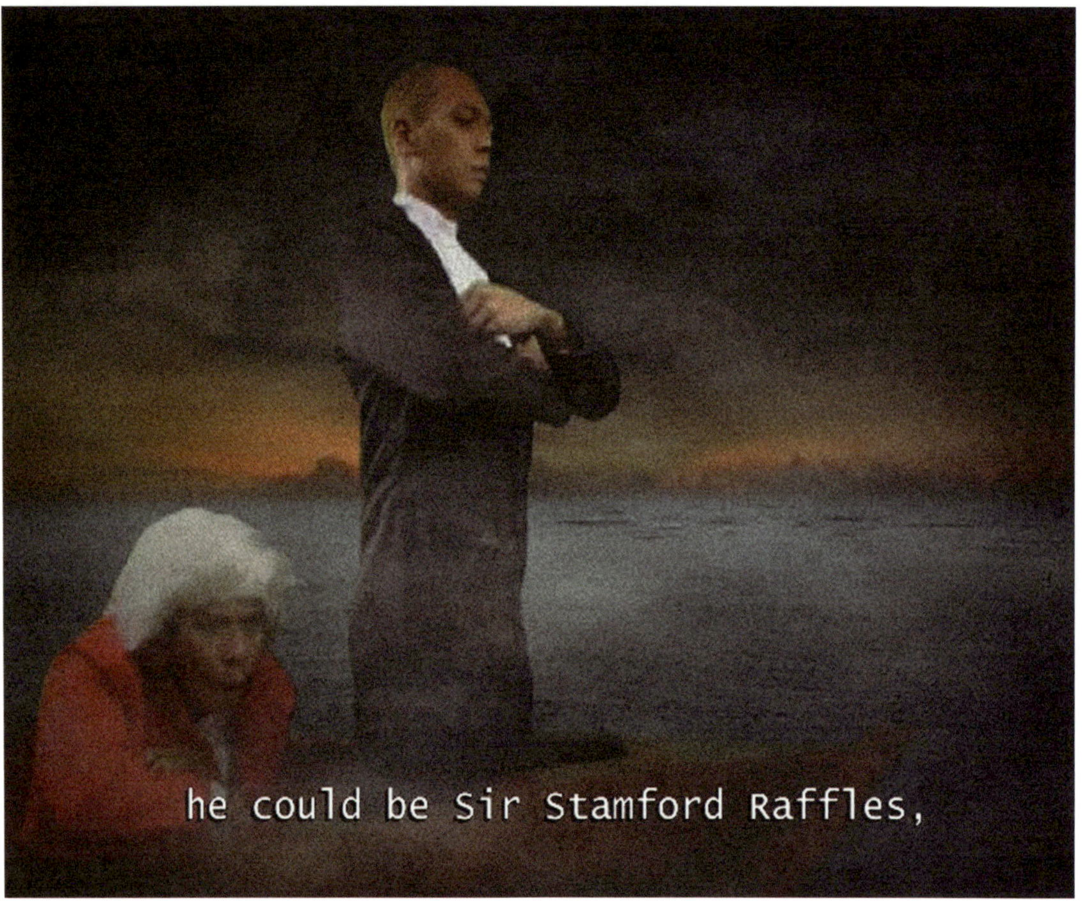

In this work, Ho Tzu Nyen fuses the historical with the imagined as he explores the question of origins and how the past is remembered. Utama draws inspiration from the legend of Sang Nila Utama, a Srivijayan prince from Palembang who founded Singhapura in the late 13th century. This work has travelled widely to art biennales and film festivals, narrating Singapore histories to a global audience.

Ho Tzu Nyen
Utama—Every Name in History is I
2003 (remade for display in 2015)
Oil on canvas; video, 23:00

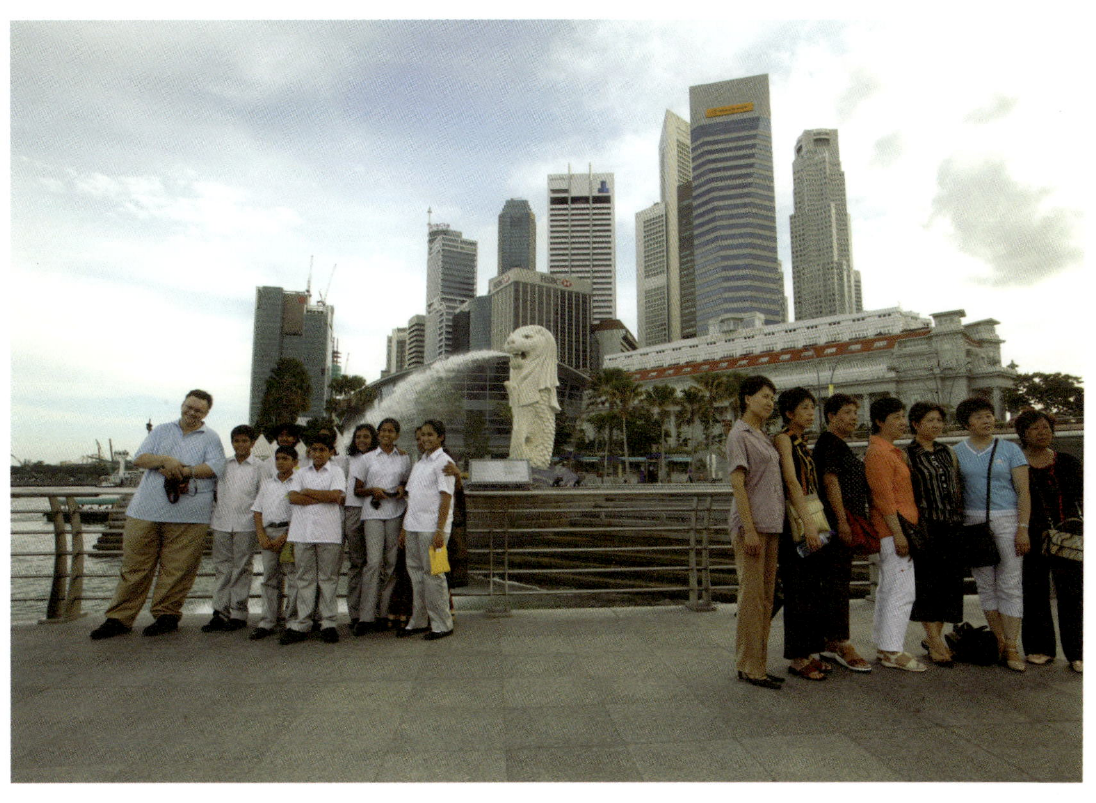

Lim Tzay Chuen
MIKE
2005
Digital print, newspaper article
33 × 48 cm
Collection of the artist